WESTERN WATERS

Fly-Fishing Memories and Lessons from Twelve Rivers

TOM ALKIRE

STACKPOLE
BOOKS
Guilford, Connecticut

Published by Stackpole Books
An imprint of The Rowman & Littlefield Publishing Group, Inc.
4501 Forbes Blvd., Ste. 200
Lanham, MD 20706
www.rowman.com

Distributed by NATIONAL BOOK NETWORK
800-462-6420

British Library Cataloguing in Publication Information available

Library of Congress Cataloging-in-Publication Data available

ISBN 978-0-8117-3829-3 (hardcover)
ISBN 978-0-8117-6872-6 (e-book)

♾ ™ The paper used in this publication meets the minimum requirements of American National Standard for Information Sciences—Permanence of Paper for Printed Library Materials, ANSI/ NISO Z39.48-1992.

Printed in the United States of America

For Dyann, Michael, and Natalie

CONTENTS

PREFACE

THANKS TO ITS RUGGED TOPOGRAPHY, THE WEST IS LACED WITH STUN-
ningly beautiful and dramatic western rivers. Too many, really. There are
too many rivers because you cannot absorb them all in a dozen lifetimes.
And when you have only one lifetime, well, you do your best.

As a fly fisherman, boater, whitewater rafter, hiker, wader, and swim-
mer, I have been immersed in rivers from my first days on the banks of the
Columbia River, the River of the West, including many of its tributaries
such as the Deschutes, Klickitat, John Day, Clark Fork, Yakima, Snake,
Grande Ronde, Kalama, and Willamette. In turn, those rivers have a web
of their own tributaries: the Clackamas, McKenzie, Blackfoot, Wallowa,
Rock Creek, and Murderer's Creek. Beyond the Columbia basin are
other western watersheds: the Klamath, Sacramento, Rogue, Umpqua,
Humboldt Sink, Colorado, Missouri, and Rio Grande. And then there
are many coastal rivers, from the Queets on the Olympic Peninsula to
Oregon's Nestucca and the Russian just north of San Francisco.

Yes, there are way too many rivers for anyone who is even halfway
awestruck by the beauty and joy of our western rivers. I have traveled
through all the western states, big sprawling states with big sprawling
rivers filled with many fishes, from sculpin to salmon to sturgeon and
especially the lovely, silvery, sleek trout: golden trout, brown trout, rainbow
trout, west slope cutthroat trout, brook trout, Apache trout, redband trout,
bull trout, sea-run cutthroat, Dolly Varden trout, and steelhead trout.

I have lived more than three score years now, and I have been fortunate to know many western rivers, some well and others not so well. And
there are many other western rivers that I have not visited but hopefully
will in the years ahead. I have known some of those rivers from the
headwaters to the sea and others only intermittently. I have camped next

to many of those rivers, fished in their cool waters, hiked up into their glacial headwaters, waded back and forth across mountain streams, and floated down desert rivers. I have been able to share those experiences with my family and friends, and I have been awed time and again by those living waters that flow by effortlessly and timelessly, year in and year out. When you spend time on a river or a particular landscape, you become intertwined with the land and waters. Today we too often separate natural history from human history, but when you spend time in a particular "place," then landscape and memory marry. Such landscapes become part of you: You may leave such a place but you never lose it.

All the rivers detailed in these pages are ones that I have been to and fished their waters, most of them over many decades and a few for only a few days. Also, I have read and studied about those rivers in front of my fireplace and in my lawn chair on the deck. And while I am no fly-fishing expert or fishing guide, I have learned a bit about these rivers and their fisheries over the years, so the chapters ahead in this book should provide some helpful information for you anglers who are ready to wade into some of these rivers and catch some fish.

Rivers and I are close friends because we share our sense of time, the slope of time, although our notion of time is ethereal and a river's notion of time is physical. Or as Henry Thoreau best said in his book *Walden*: "Time is but the stream I go a-fishing in. I drink at it: but while I drink I see the sandy bottom and detect how shallow it is. Its thin current slides away, but eternity remains." The rivers will flow on and we will not, though in a small way we sometimes can. I reflect on the camps where I have slept, the warming fires crackling against the black night, the people shadowed by the lantern's light, the rivers I have known, my drift boat anchored against swift current, the fish caught—and the ones that got away! And when those experiences find their way into my mind, my fingertips clatter across the keyboard putting words down onto the screen. Afterwards, there is something new on my table, a new life, compounding one experience upon another, rich, multi-leveled, watershed upon watershed. And that is what this book is: a river of memory about some of the fascinating western rivers that I have been fortunately able to experience.

The first section of this book is about a half-a-dozen Columbia River tributaries. The Columbia basin is an immense area, including major portions of four western states, smaller portions of three other states, and much of southeastern British Columbia. The first chapter is about steelheading on the John Day River, its wild and lonely watershed in northeast Oregon. Then come two chapters about trout fishing: one on the Deschutes River itself and another on one of its headwater lakes. Continuing on is the Sandy River, an urban river flowing from the south into the Columbia; and then the next chapter is about another steelhead river, the Klickitat River, its headwaters flowing down from the flanks of Mount Adams. Farther west is a chapter about fishing for Chinook salmon below the falls of the Willamette. And the next chapter is about the Columbia River itself.

The second section of the book is about some of the coastal rivers from the Olympic Peninsula to San Francisco Bay. Those two chapters are about rainforest rivers and their robust winter-run steelhead. The third section of the book is about some northern California rivers: one chapter is about the bedeviling Klamath River watershed with its torturous geography and politics—and its large rainbow trout. The next chapter is about the Upper Sacramento River and the headwaters of the dominating and majestic Mount Shasta.

The final section of the book is about the Rockies, an area I have visited less often but nonetheless where I have had some fine fishing on those Big Sky trout rivers. One chapter is about some Colorado rivers, the rooftop of many headwaters, some flowing into the Gulf of Mexico and others into the Gulf of California. And finally, there is a chapter about some Idaho and Montana trout rivers that flow down from the Continental Divide, too.

Some might say that I have omitted too many rivers in this list of western rivers. That may be true, but as the thirteenth-century Persian poet Rumi wrote, "When you are everywhere, you are nowhere; when you are somewhere, you are everywhere."

SECTION I

COLUMBIA TRIBUTARIES

CHAPTER ONE

Oregon Trail Steelhead

THE JOHN DAY RIVER, A TRIBUTARY OF THE COLUMBIA, IS ONE OF THE oldest river basins in the Pacific Northwest. Much of the area was inundated by an ancient sea dotted with oceanic islands that stretched to the Idaho border, basement rocks as old as 250 million years. Over time the sea receded and the continent moved westward creating the shoreline of the Pacific Ocean that we know today. Eventually, a river cut through that new landscape and we call it the John Day. At 284 miles in length, the John Day is one of the longest undammed rivers in the country, unlike the Columbia itself, which is studded with dams.

The John Day's headwaters tumble down through a welter of central and eastern Oregon mountain ranges—the Elkhorn Mountains, Blue Mountains, Strawberry Mountains, Ochoco Mountains—tracked with wolves, antelope, elk, cougar, deer, wild horses, and mountain sheep. Dozens of creeks and streams run through alpine meadows, lodgepole pine, yellow-bellied ponderosa pine, aromatic juniper, mountain-mahogany, and sagebrush. There are two Rock Creeks in the John Day watershed; other tributaries include Bridge Creek, Pine Creek, Murderer's Creek, Fox Creek, Desolation Creek, Indian Creek, Camp Creek, Dixie Creek, Skookum Creek, Sorefoot Creek, and Lonesome Creek. These and other waters flow into the three branches of the John Day and eventually empty into the Columbia. Large in size but sparsely settled, the John Day's watershed encompasses an area almost the size of New Jersey. That state has a population of nine million. By contrast, fewer than fifteen thousand people live in the John Day basin.

The free-flowing John Day has been a highway to the spawning grounds for anadromous fish such as salmon and steelhead. (Anadromous fish are born in freshwater, spend most of their lives in the sea, and return to freshwater to spawn.) This lack of dams on the river is beneficial for the fish, but on the other hand, the river nearly dries up every fall due to irrigation withdrawals where cattle ranchers grow hay and alfalfa in the valley's bottomland. Sometimes the river runs wild in the spring with snowmelt, latte colored, roiling, fast and deep, spilling over its banks, lacing through the streamside willows. A few months later—after the snowmelt is gone, the irrigated fields green, and the cattle well fed—the river becomes a scrawny little creek trickling through the middle of the riverbed, its rocks bleached by the sun, the river too shallow to float even a kayak.

For their part the salmon and steelhead have learned to wait at the confluence of the John Day and Columbia, biding their time while the rains begin in November and the water level begins to rise so the fish can begin their migration upriver through the canyon toward the distant mountains. After a few more months of swimming upriver, the fish veer off into the tributaries, spawn, and begin the cycle all over again. The fish have adapted to those conditions over the years because they are native, wild fish. No hatchery salmon or steelhead are planted in the John Day or its tributaries, unlike many other Northwest rivers where many of the fish are hatchery reared.

I have been fortunate to have been able to spend time in the John Day country in all seasons. In the summer we camp and fish for smallmouth bass with little Muddler flies in the riffles. In the fall I chase after steelhead as they migrate from the Pacific Ocean up the Columbia and into the John Day. In winter I hunt for chukar partridge, hiking in the rimrock canyon, a lonely, steep terrain where no one but hunters and cowboys ever tread. By spring I leave the steelhead alone as they enter the tributaries and seek out their natal waters to spawn.

Not too long ago in the month of November, I spent a few days on the John Day just upriver from its confluence with the Columbia. The irrigation season was over, the rains had begun, and the river level was getting high enough so steelhead were starting to move their way upstream. Still the JD, as some call it, was low enough so my friend Dick and I were able to wade across it at a ford to reach a favorite run. The ford was the same place where the Oregon Trail crossed the river on its way west. If you look hard enough, you can see the wagon ruts on the hillside to the east of the river, the remnants of thousands of pioneers in the 1840s and 1850s who had embarked in the spring from St. Louis. By late fall they were getting close to the promised land of the Willamette Valley, but they had to ford the John Day, and river crossings were always dangerous with men, women, children, horses, dogs, and oxen having to stumble along in the swift current. I find that crossing rivers is still difficult, although nowadays I have studded felt-soled wading boots and a sturdy wading staff.

The ford is just downstream at the mouth of Rock Creek, a tributary that veins its way into the uplands of rolling wheat fields, brown now in the fall but golden in summer when the wind-swept ripened wheat stalks brush across the rounded hills. The John Day's riparian zone is nothing but a few runted trees and underbrush on either side of the blue-hued river, its current languid, punctuated with an occasional tremulous stretch of riffle water. Upward from the banks rises a hillside covered with little more than sagebrush and sometimes not even that, just pebble-strewn, rocky rust-red dirt. In the summer this unyielding arid country can register triple digits on the thermometer for days at a time. Winter is usually cold and, sometimes, the slower-moving sections of the river freeze over.

I thought that the month of November would be a fine time to fish there, and I was about twenty miles upriver of the confluence at the Columbia. The gold and flame-red leaves along the banks were falling like snow, landing on the moving water, drifting downstream until they collected along the foam line and into the back eddies. The mallards were active, wings beating rapidly as they flew upriver. Two drakes bee-lined right over my head, their iridescent metallic green heads reflecting the morning sunshine.

I was wading slowly downstream trying to cast across toward the far side of the river. I was seeking a summer-run steelhead. The seven-weight, eleven-foot switch rod and shooting head did its job. My task was to coordinate the line and rod into one graceful Spey cast. Many fly-fishing steelheaders use two-handed rods nowadays because they can cast a longer line, and also it is easier to cast when the angler is up against the brush and trees. Plus, Spey casting is less fatiguing because it involves the entire upper body and not just one arm. Most JD steelhead anglers use a shooting head line with an intermediate sink-tip and a short leader. The business end of the line can include any number of flies, though the repertoire does not have to be as varied as on a trout stream. My summer-run fly box is filled with a few large bright and dark flies and also a few smaller bright and dark flies. And I think it is helpful to tie a loop of some sort onto the eye of the hook so the fly swims more naturally, such as using a Duncan's loop knot.

Out on the John Day that day, I tied on a number 6 black, silver-ribbed fly. My cast rocketed the fly out across the river, but every now and again the whole aerial assemblage collapsed into a spaghetti of line, leader, and fly. But on the whole the fly went where I intended it to go: It disappeared just below the surface and swung across the current until it tailed directly below me. Then I stripped in the running line, raised the rod, and cast out again.

This went on hour after hour after hour. To some, this repetition— step by step, cast by cast—is boring, but to others it is mesmerizing. Those with a spiritual bent might even call such fishing transcendental. Others might call it hard work. For me, I just kept wading downstream trying to land the fly close to a mid-river rock where I had a bump earlier in the day. The uplands were quiet but I could hear the chatter of the river as the water coursed over the rocky bed. I cast the fly out again. The sky-blue fly line—bright in this drab brown landscape— curled through the air and laid out onto the surface of the water, a surface that ostensibly was level from shore to shore, but in reality was slightly arched, like a paved road that is crowned at the centerline. And just beneath the river's surface was the current, flowing steady as can be. Interestingly, a river's current is the strongest just under the surface. The current slows down at the bottom due to the friction between the water and the bottom. Water cannot slip over a solid; it clings to a microscop-ically thin layer so the current slows down when it runs into the rocks at the bottom. That is why fish often like to rest near the bottom, taking it easy compared to the faster current on top.

The fly that I had cast out onto the water was drifting downstream, and at the same time my mind began drifting off, too, to a time before the days of the Oregon Trail, a time just before the War of 1812 when a Virginia-born fur trapper named John Day joined up with the Astor Expedition led by William Price Hunt for John Jacob Astor's Pacific Fur Company. The purpose of the expedition was to establish an American fur-trading post at the mouth of the Columbia River: One group was to sail around Cape Horn and the second group was to go overland. Day was among those in the overland group.

The explorers had a difficult time getting through the knot of western mountains and canyons, and eventually, Day became ill on the banks of the Snake River in 1811. Day, about forty years old then, was one of the older men. A younger man named Ramsay Crooks stayed with Day while the rest of the party continued on. It was winter by then and the two men were fortunate to be able to rest at a Shoshone village. Later the Indians moved their camp, and for a time the two men camped on the river alone even though food was scarce. By late winter the two men began hiking out of the Snake River canyon and over the snowy Blue Mountains. Cold, hungry, and lost much of the time, they apparently wandered around the headwaters of the north fork of what would later be called the John Day River. Eventually, they found the Umatilla River watershed just to the north and followed it to the Columbia where they found another friendly Indian village.

After resting, the two men began hiking westward down the south bank of the Columbia. A few days later near the mouth of the John Day River, the two men were accosted by a group of hostile Indians. The Indians stripped the men of their provisions, including their clothes. Naked and without equipment they walked back upstream to the village hoping for help. However, about the same time they looked out on the Columbia and saw a party from the Astorian group in their canoes. At last the two men were rescued and they traveled together down to the newly established fort at Astoria.

A few months later some of the group, including Day, began paddling their way back upstream on the Columbia seeking furs. Day's long, torturous ordeal of crossing the mountains appeared to have altered his once cheerful personality. According to several sources, Day's behavior became increasingly strange and restless as the flotilla of canoes paddled upriver. Day apparently tried to commit suicide but was unsuccessful. The party decided to send Day back to Astoria with some friendly Indians. Day remained on the coast for a while, but eventually traveled back to the Snake River country, where he died in 1819 or 1820.

Day's name was eventually placed on the map of the river that he had discovered. Plus, a river in Clatsop County, which enters the Columbia about fifteen miles from the Pacific Ocean, also is named for him. Today John Day is the name of the largest city in that region. There is also another nearby town, Dayville, named in his honor. And one of the large Columbia River hydroelectric dams on the Oregon-Washington border bears his name, too.

While Day discovered "his" river, he did not really examine it very closely, because at the time he was lost, naked, cold, and hungry. It was not until fifteen years later that another group of trappers more thoroughly explored the John Day basin, this time not from an American expedition, but from the British Hudson's Bay Company. For most of the first half of the nineteenth century, the Pacific Northwest was jointly occupied by the two nations. The British were concerned that more and more Americans might be coming through the Oregon Country and would overwhelm the British settlements in the Northwest. By the 1820s the company implemented a policy to exterminate the fur bearers, primarily beaver, south and east of the Columbia River, so with the fur trade gone, the rival American fur companies would turn back.

Peter Skene Ogden and his expedition tried their best to execute the company's policy, and they explored much of the inter-mountain West, including the John Day basin. However, in 1826 Ogden recorded that the Northern Paiutes already had trapped out most of the beavers in the John Day basin. In a few more decades, beavers were almost totally extirpated in the area. While the British were successful in wiping out the beaver, they were unsuccessful stemming the flow of

Americans going westward. By the time the two nations resolved the ownership of the area in 1846, the boundary was established far north of the banks of the Columbia River.

Today the beavers are back, re-establishing in some tributaries along the John Day. In fact, government agencies are putting out the welcome mat for beavers because in many places beaver dams and ponds are beneficial to salmon and steelhead spawning and rearing. I have seen the evidence of such beaver activity—telltale pointed tree stumps—on the John Day and other rivers.

After all this remembering, my mind drifted back into focus once again and I waded downriver a step or two. I looked up the river and saw Dick casting rhythmically across and down the current, the water up to his knees, his stance intent. Across the river there were some spin-anglers and I noticed that one of them had a steelhead on the line. I was some thirty yards away and could get a decent view of their tackle and modus operandi. I surmised that they were using shrimp and bobbers, which are legal, even though all the wild fish are required to be released. Some twenty minutes later I saw another bait-angler catch and release another fish.

"So the steelhead are there," I said to myself. It was only a question of whether or not the fish wanted to take a fly. The most effective way to catch fish is usually with bait, but fishing with a fly is more fun—at least to me.

As I coaxed the fly closer into the sweet spot, I tightened up. Even though I was fishing—and fishing is supposed to be relaxing—still I was tense. I had been relaxed earlier: the inviting blue-green color of the water, its white chop over the slick rocks, the darkness of its pools, the banks thick with willows and grasses, the bright sharp autumnal sky. But now I was tight as a drum, yearning, hoping that I would connect with something wild. The contemplative man, the Izaak Walton type of man, had vanished and in its place was the alert man, expectant, ready to pounce.

Then I saw the swirl out in front of me. I looked at my line to see if the swirl was related to where the line was, and before I could say yes, I noticed that the line began to tighten. It was not an instant strike as are some strikes. It was a slow take, maybe a hesitant fish, rubbing the fly along its jawline, wondering whether or not it should open its mouth and bite down on it.

Another second and there was no mistake about it: The fish was fast to my line and it was tugging, swirling on the surface, splashing all over the place. Next I saw its rose-red flank as it jumped out of the water, the drops in the air sparkling in the sunshine, the fish's silver body brilliant against a backdrop of a crisp fall sky. I was there, totally aware, eyes wide open, mind laser-concentrated, no multitasking, all aboard, mind on the water. I was there, knee-deep in the river, right there, not over there, or back there, or there over on the other side, but there.

"Yes, Izaak, I'm in the moment, present tense, a hundred percent there."

The contemplative fly fisherman, mellow and calm, had morphed into a thrill seeker, the adrenaline surging through my body, its cardiac output ballistic.

From the fish's point of view, it was simply trying to get away from that damn sharp piece of metal and was pulling against something unknown and unseen. Maybe the fish had struck at the fly because it "thought" that it was a morsel of food, or maybe it was just ornery and slapped at that little feathery son-of-a-gun as it swung through the current, or maybe it was bored and wanted to chase something small and bright. Maybe, maybe. We will never know. There are a thousand suppositions about why a fish bites down on little more than a metal hook, a few feathers, and a dab of fur.

Had I been catching fish all day long and the day before that and the day before that, I would not have had the same sensation; but the hookup was exciting because many of us steelheaders often spend hours upon hours of casting—maybe days—before they get into a fish, so when you do get the Big Pull, you do not take it for granted.

Poof!

The line went slack and the bow in the rod was gone. There was no splashing at the end of the line, just the current flowing along, just as it did yesterday and as it would tomorrow. Whereas a moment before my mind and body were totally energized, now there was nothing: The air didn't just leak out of the tire; it was a blowout. I reeled in some line thinking that maybe the fish had run upstream and thereby the line was slack because of that. Sometimes that happens, and it is always a relief after you have reeled in some line and realize that the fish is still on.

No luck this time. Wherever the fish was now—licking its wounds, maybe resting in the lee of a boulder—it was not connected to my line. The fish had apparently thrown the hook—maybe when it jumped. Or maybe the point of the hook just barely penetrated the fish's bony jaw and fell out as the pull of the line tightened. Or maybe the fly was never solidly hooked. Or . . .

After I retrieved the fly, I examined it and did not see anything amiss. I scratched the point of the hook against my fingernail and found its telltale track across my nail, making me think that the hook was sharp.

Whatever it was, the fish was gone. I would have liked to have played the fish and landed it, of course, but at least I experienced the Big Tug once again. There is a tremendous difference between hooking a fish— even briefly—and not hooking a fish at all. You don't always get what you want, but sometimes you get what you need.

One year later Dick and I returned to the exact same spot. The river level was much the same as it was the year before. On our first day of fishing, Dick landed a very nice fish. On the second day I tied on my Midnight Fire, a rubber-legged fly, onto the end of my ten-pound tippet. The day before I had not touched anything—not even a bump—and so by mid-morning I started to get into a funk, for I wanted something to happen . . . something . . .

"Yo!" I said to myself as the rod jerked violently.

The fish ran straight toward me putting slack line all over the water. I assumed that the fish was going to shake the hook out of its mouth, because the line was no longer taut. Then, with line all over the water, the fish suddenly turned and ran back upstream and out into mid-stream. The line held. I could not believe it. And then it jumped . . . way out of the water. It laid out horizontally above the river, its tail slapping the air. It was a foot or two above the surface. It flopped back into the water and then did the same thing again, apparently wanting to be in the air rather than in the water.

Dick was fishing just upstream of me and could see the fish jumping. "Five . . . six . . . ," yelled Dick, who counted out the number of the fish's jumps.

By number nine the fish finally started to tire. I reeled the line in and brought the fish close to the bank; the fish saw me and bolted. Finally, I was able to coax it into the shallows once again. Most John Day steelhead are relatively small, between three to five pounds. However, some steelhead in the John Day are not native to the John Day. The other steelhead in the river somehow ventured into the John Day and are called strays because they originated from other Columbia tributaries. My fish appeared to be a stray as it was much larger than a typical JD fish, probably about ten pounds. I assumed it was a Clearwater fish, for they are known for their size. Located in Idaho, the Clearwater River is a tributary of the Snake River, which, in turn, is the largest tributary of the Columbia.

I noticed that the adipose fin was intact, so it was a wild fish and I was going to release it. Better said than done, however. The fish must have struck hard when it attacked that dark fly—its rubber legs titillating, twitching in the current. I grasped the jaws of my pliers onto the bend of the hook and had to struggle to get it out: nothing but steel and bone. Finally, I backed the fly out at just the right angle and the fly slid out safely. I tailed the big fish in the water so it could rest: I could see its gill plates "breathing" back and forth in the oxygenated water. It was a splendid fish with a pink-blushed stripe on its flanks and a dark olive color on its top. In a few minutes the fish flexed its strong tail, pushed my fingers away, and swam out into the deeper water.

Satisfied?

Oh, yes . . . yes, indeed.

I walked back upstream to fish a little more, but before long I decided to wade back across the river and go back to the car because it was nearly noon and there was food in the cooler. Also, I was satiated for the moment and did not have the concentration required to get that fly back into the river properly. I hiked along the bank and looked up at the brown and tan hills. The draws were thick with sagebrush, tumbleweeds, and wild rose. Upwards the terrain got steeper, the vegetation sparse, just a few shafts of cheatgrass, like the thinning hair on a man's bald head. And farther upslope there was no vegetation at all, just rock talus—broken, brown, basalt shards that clatter like broken glass when you step onto the precarious angular slope, or what the geologists call the angle of repose. I could not guess the degree of the angle on that particular talus slope, for it depends on the type of rock. Whatever the angle was, the rock was for the moment stationary, but it does not take much for such a rock pile to begin moving, for it always appears to be on the verge of sliding. There is a tension to such rocky slopes, a tension between friction and gravity, and sometimes you can hear the sound of gravity at work. More than once I have traversed a steep riverbank and suddenly heard the clatter of moving rock. It is always a bit unnerving when that happens, but such is gravity, that omnipresent force that attracts all things toward the center of the Earth.

Farther upriver the John Day begins to split into several forks that go up into the mountains: the North Fork, South Fork, and the main stem. All these branches have their own headwaters, tributary streams that rush down the river in the spring with the snowmelt. By late summer many of these streams will be dry. The longest branch of the John Day—and the largest one by volume, too—is the North Fork, and it snakes its way east of the fossil country up into the timberland, into the Greenhorn Mountains and Elkhorn Mountains with peaks as high as nine thousand feet. Some of the headwaters of the North Fork are in a federally designated wilderness area. These waters and those of the Middle Fork of the North Fork were first discovered by gold miners in the late nineteenth century, but that activity has long since ceased, and the once bustling mining camps are nothing but ghost towns: once a wilderness, then a hub of commerce, and then wilderness again, so goes the John Day headwaters.

The mountains there are thinly forested with ponderosa pine and lodgepole pine. The country is populated with deer, elk, cougars, wolves, coyotes, mountain goats, ruffed grouse, blue grouse, and waterfowl. The John Day headwaters include dozens of nursery streams for salmon and steelhead. Born in those cold waters, they rear for a year or so in the mountain streams and then they go out to the sea. There they feed in the ocean pasture and later return to their natal spawning grounds. Undammed and with clear cold water, the John Day has one of the larger populations of wild Chinook salmon and wild steelhead in the Columbia basin. In the upper reaches of the river and its tributaries, the Chinook and steelhead relentlessly push upriver to their spawning grounds, at times their bellies scraping against the bottom of the substrate as they search out the best spawning water. The steelhead, which are anadromous rainbow trout, sometimes are able to spawn and then return to the ocean and spawn a second time. The salmon do not return to the ocean. They have traveled some four hundred miles from the mouth of the Columbia to the headwaters of the John Day. By the time they are in their spawning waters, they are discolored, weak, white fungus on their fins and tails. They listlessly drift downstream, their carcasses beached in the shallows, bald eagles poking at their rotting flesh. A few weeks later the eggs will hatch and the tiny alevin will begin their journey all over again.

Away from the river's spawning waters are steep hills that fold one upon another as they rise higher and higher toward the crest. There are few paved roads in this area. There are some dirt roads nearby for sure, but none at all within the boundary of the wilderness area. This terrain is stunningly beautiful with snowy-edged mountaintops and deeply cleaved canyons. Few people travel in that country as it is a long way from any major populated area. Most people who pass through the John Day River headwaters drive on US Highway 395, a scenic north-south route that links Spokane, Washington, to San Bernardino, California. And the busiest time of year in this area is during deer- and elk-hunting season, for hunters from around the country seek out those animals in the upper reaches of the John Day basin.

I myself have hunted for deer in that country. I recall one late afternoon that I was on a stand on a ridge looking out toward the North Fork where it flowed out of the wilderness area. I pulled my hat brim down onto my forehead and shielded my eyes as I was looking uplight, toward the sun, a blindingly bright orange ball against the October sky. A ruffed grouse suddenly exploded out of a bush and scared the daylights out of me. I settled back down on a stump and put my rifle across my lap. I took a sip of water out of the canteen and zipped up my blaze orange vest as the temperature was cooling down by the minute. I took the binoculars up to my eyes and scanned the hillside, hoping a buck mule deer might sneak out of its daytime hide, ready to feed on twigs and leaves in the green-up patches along the snarly little creek.

The sun's descent over the western horizon had a sense of grace to it as a pale moon also rose in the east, the two luminaries facing one another. Soon the golden disc dropped down below the horizon entirely, gone but still alive in its own way, inflaming the colors of a Blue Mountains sunset. I glassed more intently than ever, the binoculars picking up more light than would be possible with the naked eye. Gradually, the light grew weaker and weaker, and eventually, I had to put the binoculars away and stuff them back in my daypack. Finally, I picked up the pack and put a flashlight in my hand. I put the leather sling and rifle over my shoulder and hiked down a game trail to the car a mile away. By then the sky had darkened even more. In most areas of the country, the lights of the civilized world would have started to twinkle—ranches with their electric lights dotting the landscape, street lights in small towns, farmhouses, outbuildings, highway roadside gasoline stations. As I continued down the hill—my boots treading carefully so as not to trip on the rough basalt shards—the only light I saw was the beam of my flashlight. I thought of Homer, who wrote in *The Odyssey* more than two thousand years ago: "The sun sank and the roads of the world grew dark."

A friend of mine visited Tokyo not long ago and had a conversation with a Japanese friend about the population densities in different places. My friend tried to tell his Japanese friend about places like eastern Oregon with its sparse human population. The conversation was not easy with the language difficulty and the conversion from miles into kilometers, but eventually, the two of them determined the geographical facts of life. The John Day River watershed has a population density of about five people per square mile. To the Japanese man, this was incomprehensible because Japan has a population density of about eight hundred people per square mile.

So goes the John Day River and its sparse watershed—sparsely peopled, sparsely vegetated, and sparsely watered. In much of the region, its population was greater years ago, but mining and logging have played out and the mechanization of agriculture has reduced the number of farmworkers as well. The North Fork headwaters town of Granite had a population of 250 in 1901. It has thirty-eight today. The nearby town of Greenhorn is on the divide between the John Day River and Snake River drainages at an elevation of sixty-three hundred feet. It had twice the population of Granite back in the day. Now Greenhorn is still an incorporated city but it has a population of zero.

Who knows, things may change in the John Day basin, but for now its closest city lights are a long way away.

CHAPTER TWO

A River in a Land of Lava

MANY RIVERS FROM THE BRITISH COLUMBIA BORDER TO NORTHERN California are etched into a landscape of lava. From eighteen million years to ten million years ago, molten lava squeezed out through the cracks of the Earth and onto the plains of the interior Pacific Northwest. Lava flowed across the landscape like floodwaters across the pasture lands: the lava, viscous like mercury, half liquid half solid, hissing, steaming up into the gnarly gray thickened air; the lava, cooling, the orange glow blackening by the minute, solidifying itself, rough and raw, twisting into the basaltic formations that we see today. Those floodwaters of fire spread across the landscape and before long the basalt was thick upon the Earth.

After a few more million years, tectonic forces went to work and the Cascade Range emerged—still restless, magma bubbling at the base of the newly formed volcanoes. Some of those volcanoes erupted and some were catastrophic, such as the one at Mount Mazama some seventy-seven hundred years ago that blew the top off the mountain and created Crater Lake. More recently to the north was the Mount St. Helens eruption of 1980 that blew out the north face of what once was the most symmetrical snowcap peak of the entire Cascades.

In what is now called central Oregon, there was a river that originally flowed westward out toward the Pacific Ocean, but the north-south orientation of the newly built Cascades Range blocked the river. As all rivers do when confronting an obstacle, the river changed its course. Rivers are not stupid: They know what to do. Blocked by the mountains to the west, the river headed north toward the Columbia River and began slicing through the newly formed lava. Water may appear soft and pliable compared to rock, but gravity can do wonders and before long the river started to cut through the fire-born basalt hour by hour, century by century. That river is the 250-mile-long Deschutes River, and it drains the eastern slope of the Cascades from south of the city of Bend all the way north to the Columbia River. To the east of the river is one of its major tributaries, the Crooked River, which has a large basin itself, including much of the Ochoco Mountains and Maury Mountains. All total, the Deschutes River and its tributaries drain an area the size of Massachusetts.

And the headwaters?

The source of the Deschutes is not as obvious as are some other rivers. Ostensibly, the source of the Deschutes is Little Lava Lake. But that is the *visible* source of the river. As a land of lava, the source of the river is more a sponge than a pinpoint. Just a few miles north of Little Lava Lake is Elk Lake. The waters in that lake flow underground downhill and end up in Little Lava, so is Elk Lake the source? Moreover, a number of nearby tributaries, such as the Metolius River and the Fall River, have their headwaters as hidden springs. Those rivers do not gradually start out as rills and creeks: Those rivers simply become. They are just there. Their cold waters bubble out of the ground, and presto—a river. I've watched both rivers become full-grown rivers in an instant: Under the pines and scruffy underbrush, a spring suddenly appears, gurgling, cold, clean water, day in and day out, summer and winter.

And where does that water in those springs emanate from? It comes from rain and melted snow in the high country that percolate down into the porous soil and migrate through the underground cracks in the lava beds. Volcanic activities over the years created many faults and fissures where water can flow back and forth under the ground. In turn, some of that water sloshing around beneath the surface rises to the top. Actually, very little of the planet's freshwater is located above ground. The rivers that we actually see are a small fraction of the waters that lie below the surface. Call them aquifers or subterranean rivers, Earth's underground waters lie hidden from us and only spring forth from time to time.

The land of lava is filled with lava tubes and fissures. Some of the most recent lava flows are in the upper reaches of the Deschutes basin along the eastern slope of the Cascades. It is a land of naked lava, all helter-skelter in some places and orderly in other places like the soldierly columnar basalt. The Deschutes gradually cut through that newly minted lava land, and the canyon it created was steep walled and the river relatively straight. Old rivers have oxbows and meanders. Young rivers do not have time for such dallying. The Deschutes has not had time yet to stretch out its watercourse and create floodplains and bottomland. By contrast, the John Day River has had more time to go to work, and as a result, it has a wider canyon than does the Deschutes. There are many more acres of bottomland with ranches and pastures along the John Day than on the Deschutes. The Deschutes's gradient is steeper too and has more rapids than does the John Day.

The Deschutes canyon has largely been an impediment to transportation and not the other way around as is typical for many rivers, such as the Columbia, which has been a major water transportation network ever since the Indian days. The Lewis and Clark Expedition paddled its canoes up and down the Columbia, and so did the fur traders later on. They transported tons of beaver pelts and other cargo along the Columbia and its tributaries. Before too long, steamships began piloting up the river from the Columbia's mouth all the way as far as southern British Columbia. The Willamette River was the main avenue of commerce for much of the nineteenth century from Portland to Eugene until the railroads arrived, and even today the river is a major commercial port in its lower reaches. And back in the day, small paddle-wheeled steamships navigated up and down the John Day River in high-water months.

But on the Deschutes the steep canyons, rough rapids, and waterfalls precluded commercial water transport. Just getting across the river from one side to the other has been difficult from the get-go. The earliest explorer who saw the Deschutes River was once again Peter Skene Ogden, the Hudson's Bay Company fur trapper who roamed across a wide swath of the West. His 1825 expedition traveled up the west bank of the Deschutes from the mouth to Dry Creek, a few miles north of the present-day town of Warm Springs. There his party crossed the

Deschutes on the way to find better fur country to the east. They made it across, but they lost four horses in the process.

Today there is a broad gravel bar just downstream of Dry Creek where anglers can wade out halfway across the river. I have anchored my boat on that bar many times and fished that water. I have always wondered if that is where Ogden and his party crossed. I certainly would not try to cross the river there, but I did not have a horse along either. But then again, likely the river has changed substantially since Ogden's men rode their horses down to the bank and into the river. It was a very different time, too, for John Quincy Adams was president then and the Pacific Northwest was still unmapped and unclaimed.

After the fur traders left came the miners who wanted to reach the gold fields in the upper John Day country, but they had to cross the Deschutes canyon to get there. One of the most likely crossings was at Sherars Falls, a traditional Indian salmon-fishing site, some forty miles upstream from the mouth of the Columbia. John Todd built a wooden toll bridge there in 1860 just below the falls. A decade later Joseph Sherars purchased the bridge and improved the wagon road on either side of the bridge. He and his wife built a hotel and stagecoach station near the bridge, and they operated it until their deaths in 1907 and 1908, respectively. Soon after the railroad line was completed up through the canyon, the bridge and its hotel became less and less important. Eventually, the old wooden bridge was replaced with a toll-free concrete bridge and the buildings were demolished. Sherars Falls itself remains much the same, of course, oblivious as always to the comings and goings of us humans.

Even today there are few bridges on the lower Deschutes. The Sherars Falls Bridge is the first bridge upriver from the mouth. Next there is a highway bridge across the river at the town of Maupin. Upstream of that is the US Highway 26 bridge at Warm Spring almost one hundred miles from the mouth.

There are several railroad bridges that cross the Deschutes, too. The tracks run up the canyon from the mouth of the river to Trout Creek, where the line comes out of the canyon and up onto the flatland to Gateway and beyond. To those of us who camp along the banks of the river, a midnight freight train rolling along some thirty feet away is not something you sleep through. Usually, I feel the approaching train first, tremors beneath the darkened ground. Each locomotive weighs over one hundred tons and fully loaded railcars can weigh almost as much, too, so it is not surprising that a person feels the vibrations of a moving train when you are sleeping on the ground. To the uninitiated, it feels as though the terra firma below your ground cloth is not as firma as you think it is. To me, the sensation of being on the ground, close to a moving freight train, feels not unlike an earthquake, where once solid ground is no longer solid, where the Earth is tenuous at best. The locomotive's headlamp illuminates the dark canyon, bathing the blackness with a ghostly, lonely whiteness. Sometimes it is difficult to ascertain where the train is coming from—upcanyon or downcanyon. When the train finally does rumble by, the noise is deafening, the clickety-clack, the desert air rushing by . . . and then . . . it's gone . . . in a few minutes the silence of the night creeps back in, deafening in its own way, the camp once again stilled, a lustrous sheen on the river's surface illuminated by the light of the moon.

Until the early 1970s there were few boats on the river. And then along came the recreational boating boom that continues today. On any summer weekend in the lower Deschutes, you will find thousands of people stuffed into various boats: some looking for whitewater fun, others for the fishing, and still others for the simple enjoyment of the river itself and its spectacular canyon. Early on the boats on the Deschutes were wooden rowboats and canoes. But by the late 1900s the boat manufacturers went to work and created a wide variety of whitewater vessels, including kayaks, inflatable rafts, pontoon boats, drift boats, and jet boats. I have been in all of these types of boats and each of them has their own purpose. My favorite, of course, is the drift boat, a graceful boat with a husky upturned bow, low-profiled broad midsection, and a narrow upturned stern. Originated in the Pacific Northwest to navigate whitewater rivers, drift boats are now made of wood, aluminum, and fiberglass. The drift boat captain is also the oarsman who is stationed in the middle seat and uses two long oars. The boat "drifts" down the river, without a motor, and the oarsman steers the boat, trying to avoid rocks, whirlpools, debris, and shallow gravel bars. If pointed downstream, the bow will slide up and over the wave crests easily. If turned sideways to the current, the waves might curl those whitecaps right over the top of the gunwale and into your lap.

"Keep the bow towards trouble so you can pull away from it," said my friend Bill Bakke years ago when I first learned how to row a drift boat.

The drift boat is a fishing boat that can negotiate rough and tumble western rivers. I cannot remember how many times I have taken my sixteen-foot fiberglass drift boat down the Deschutes. Not enough, you might say. Every boat owner gets attached to his or her boat. Though an inanimate object, the boat seems almost alive when it slides into the water once again after being strapped on to the trailer for months at a time. Like a bird dog that gets excited when it bounds out of the car and steps out into a brushy field ready to hunt, so the boat enlivens itself when it gets on the water, its smooth hull wetted, the river lapping at the boat's waterline.

"Finally!"

The Deschutes is the highway and the boat the vehicle. Modes of transport always have an endearing relationship between the operator and the vehicle, whether it is a boat, car, or plane. In the case of my drift boat, when I sit down onto the rowing bench, the boat and I become one unit, like horse and rider. Together we can accomplish great feats of transportation. In the beginning when I purchased the boat, my drift boat rowing skills were rudimentary, but I learned quickly. The boat was always ready to do fine things, but it could not steer by itself. Eventually, I learned that if I lined up the boat properly, the boat would do what it was meant to do. When things go haywire it is never because of the boat: It is because of the operator. Scores of drift boats float down the Deschutes every day in the summer and fall. There are boating accidents, some serious, from time to time on those waters, but I have never heard that it was because of the boat.

There are few roads along the lower Deschutes, and so a boat is critical to reach the best fishing spots. Oddly, the Deschutes is one of the few rivers where it is illegal to actually fish out of a boat: You have to anchor on a gravel bar or pull up on the shore and then get out and wade to fish. The Deschutes is a good-sized river and wading is out of reach in many places. As a result, the Deschutes's native rainbow trout, called redsides, have a natural refuge where they are safe from at least human predators. This arrangement appears to have worked well over the decades as the trout reproduce successfully year after year. The fish are healthy and measure up to twenty inches and some larger. However, these wild fish are wily and not easily caught. Bait is not allowed on the lower Deschutes so most anglers use fly-fishing gear. Finding out how, where, and when to use the right fly to catch a Deschutes redside is always a challenge.

Many small-stream fly anglers who first come to the Deschutes are intimidated by its size and its rough and tumble flow. I tell them not to worry. The best trout lies are often in close to the banks. In most cases, anglers do not have to wade halfway out into the strong current. In fact, I have seen more than one angler who has barged through the bushes and splashed into the river as he plowed his way out into the main flow. Well, those trout that *had* been finning in next to the grasses and under the alder trees ... well ... they are long gone. Heck, I have caught large trout in very shallow water beneath the undercut banks. The alert fish watches the bugs sliding by with the current as it flows by under the overhanging grasses. The fish, protected by the undercut bank, darts out from its little underwater den and takes a fluttering salmonfly or maybe a blue-wing olive mayfly. The bankside angler hoping for a hookup can stealthily dab a fly out onto the water right next to the edge of the bank, or he can wade out into the river and cast the fly back in toward the bank. Both methods work.

Also, there are many islands on the river, and the timid angler can sometimes make a big river into a small one by fishing the inside channel of the island. (Note: Some of the islands bordering the Warm Springs Reservation are off limits to fishing.) The river's terrain is arid with few trees, and so in the summer months it is best to try to find areas where the river is shadowed a bit because that is where the fish feel most protected. This is especially true during the steelhead season in the summer and early fall. Steelhead—and trout—do not have eyelids and usually sulk down to the bottom when the sun shines on the water. (See more about summer-run steelhead fly fishing in chapters 1 and 5.)

The Deschutes rainbow trout feed primarily on aquatic insects, bugs that live mostly *in* the water. Near the end of their lives, the bugs metamorphose and spend their remaining days flying around in the air searching for mates. The main groups of those insects include stoneflies, caddisflies, midges, and mayflies. Seldom observed by non-anglers, these underwater insects are the basic building blocks of a productive, healthy environment that nourishes trout, frogs, swallows, and—through the Great Chain of Being—the angler himself.

Aquatic insects "hatch" most often in the warmer months when the nymphs or pupae swim up to the surface and emerge into a winged adult. Sometimes these airborne insects emerge by the thousands and the trout slurp them up by the mouthful. Of course, the fly angler tries to figure out the appropriate insect that the fish are feeding upon so the angler, in turn, can tie on an imitation of that particular bug. Anglers call this matching the hatch. It is easier said than done. The Deschutes is not the best dry fly–fishing river, though anglers catch a lot of fish on dries using Blue-Wing-Olives, Elk Hair Caddis, and salmonfly imitations. But when an obvious hatch is not in process, it is usually best to do some nymph fishing, using maybe a Flashback Pheasant Tail or Gold-Ribbed Hare's Ear or any number of nymphs and emergers.

One of the most obvious hatches on the Deschutes is the salmonfly hatch. Anglers like the salmonfly hatch because the trout love to eat those large bugs. The artificial flies that resemble the salmonfly are large, too; they are easy to see on the water and anglers like that, as well. These insects first live several years underwater as nymphs in the fast riffles before migrating to the shore where they break out of their outer coverings, or exoskeletons. Measuring as large as two inches long with a salmon-red underbelly and veined gray wings, the adult salmonflies cluster on the tall grasses and bushes along the river's edge. They are clumsy fliers, fall into the water easily, and end up in the mouths of trout quite often.

I remember one May years ago when my friend Chris and I camped below Beavertail hoping to find the salmonfly hatch going on. After we got our camp squared away, we hauled a small rubber raft to the shore and then crossed it to a large island. The wedge of land midstream was alive with red-winged blackbirds, doves, and meadowlarks. It was alive too with more than a dozen large cedar trees, an anomaly in this parched landscape of basalt rimrock, sagebrush, and juniper, the scented mnemonic berries that give the area its aroma. Underfoot were clumps of five-petal, magenta-colored flowers, small and wispy between the towering clumps of sage and the dried, ghostlike Russian thistles.

I waded slowly upstream on the outside channel of the island. I cast a number 6 Bullet-Head Salmonfly in next to the bushes. Large and easy to follow on the drift, the fly sparked little interest after several efforts. Then there was a bit of a swirl, but it was only a small fish. After a while there was a splash next to the fly and suddenly a fish was on. It was not a large one, but it was an active one. I brought the fish to hand and then released it. I waded upstream and cast out toward the bank again and again. Zip. I changed flies and tied on a Golden Stonefly because I had seen more goldens on the grasses than salmonflies. Perhaps the salmonfly hatch was over. Usually, the golden stonefly hatches come next and after that come the little yellow stones, but you never know.

The adult Golden Stonefly did not work out well so I tied on a weighted golden nymph. I have been told that trout feed madly on crawling stonefly nymphs as they lumber along from rock to rock on the river's bottom, driven by the urge to shuck their exoskeletons and emerge as airborne adults. After I lobbed the heavy fly into the riffles for a while, I had a suspicion that the migration of the goldens was over, too.

I looked into the warming morning air and noticed a few small caddisflies in the air. I then tied on a Gold-Ribbed Hare's Ear, a useful jack-of-all-trades type nymph. Made out of drab-colored fur and usually weighted, the Hare's Ear has been around for several hundred years and the variations are endless. After several casts I still did not see much action.

"Kinda slow for me," said Chris as he walked over toward me.

"Me too," I said. I reeled in the fly, climbed up the bank, and we hiked over to the inside of the channel and took the raft back to camp to have lunch and rest until the evening rise.

As the light began to fade over the waters, we put our waders back on and headed to the river. Evenings seem endless on the summertime Deschutes, when the sun drops behind the canyon's western rim leaving a soft light that fades ever so slowly into night, the air thickening with bugs, the sky glowing rosy and mauve against the rusted brown cliffs. We leapfrogged down the bank of the river from one hopeful spot to the next.

I tied on a number 16 green-bellied Elk Hair Caddis and rubbed a bit of floatant on it. I stepped into the river and slowly began working upstream hard up against the banks a few feet from shore. Every now and again I hooked a fish, but most of them were small. I wanted a larger fish, not a trophy, just what I call a meaningful trout, one that should have a bit of heft to it and be able to run some line off the spool.

I waded over to the bank and grabbed a large caddis off one of the alder leaves and noticed its reddish body color, swept-back wings, and two long antennae. Then I noticed another one. And another. I switched flies and tied on a number 10 red-bodied Bucktail Caddis.

Matched the hatch. Found the range. Couldn't keep the fish off. Suddenly, for once, there was strike after strike. The fish were not large, but they were strong and meaningful for sure, maybe fourteen inches or so. Now and again I saw them rise from beneath the surface, rocket toward the fly, and then attack it. Wonderful, deep-bodied redsides, silver flanks with a pink-blushed lateral line running right into the gill plates. Four, then five hookups and then I lost track. I was delighted, for such action does not happen often, at least to me.

The fishing slowed down as it always eventually does. I worked upstream looking for the right water: swift but still flat, no chop, two to four feet deep between the shore and the shoulder of the whitewater, broken by boulders and logs. Ahead I could see them rising—dimples on the darkening water, slurps of feeding trout pressed against a bug-ridden sky. The day was about coming to a close, never to be again; I wanted to hold on to it, put my arms around it, keep the present present and not have it fade into the past. Darker and darker was the evening light, and finally I could not follow the fly as it drifted down the current. The constant upstream wading had turned my legs to rubber, and I climbed out of the water and plodded up the steep bank trying to avoid the patches of poison sumac. I thrust my wading staff in between the rocks of the talus slope and pulled myself up, foot by foot.

Before long Chris and I had gotten out of our waders and were drinking beer and cooking steaks. Soon the two tired anglers were lying down in their respective tents, consciousness fading into a cricket-chorused night dusted with stars. A breeze sifted its way through and around the camp gear and everything else. And in the dead of night, the breeze would die down, and by first light the invisible water vapor in the air would cool and condense and the leaves and grasses would be wet with dew, the dawn weak, shy, its color a dour gray at first and gradually pink, violet, gold, and orange. As novelist Willa Cather best said about the western dawn in *O Pioneers!*: "like the light from some great fire that was burning under the edge of the world."

Mornings in camp alongside of the Deschutes are some of my fondest memories. Places, after all, are not only physical places but they are places in the mind, too. When you go to a place often enough, it becomes part of you: the sagebrush, wild rose, riverside alders, pungent juniper aroma, clattering rapids, fluttering caddisflies, twisted basalt columns rising from the river's shore up to the jagged edge of the sky, a sky bereft of clouds, wild with a refulgent blue. Such is the touch and smell and look of a place, but when you go there time after time, leave it and return to it again and again, then the place becomes a place in the mind, ethereal, intangible, yet absolutely real. You leave a place but you never lose it.

Of course, what makes a place especially rich are the people—family and friends who for me have been infused with the land and the waters of the Deschutes. The memories of those people, some living and others not, all live in my imagination. They never die. In that place, in my Deschutes camp, I can see my friends—Bill, Chris, Fred, Michael, Frank, Tad, Mike, Mark—at Mecca, High Camp, Rattlesnake, Ferry Canyon, Wagonblast. I can see my children when they were young, floating down the river in my drift boat toward Trout Creek; later my son scooting through Boxcar Rapids in his kayak; and later my wife and daughter waving at the engineer in the speeding locomotive while our raft floats down the river past Sinamox, a wide spot in the road where a ferry once operated. An empty land is timeless, but a land filled with people is no longer timeless. My Deschutes camp of the mind flows back and forth through time. All those people at my camp are ghosts for they were there *then*, then when we were all together, then when we cooked on the Coleman stove, set up camp, broke camp, and floated down the river. Since those moments they have moved on, but they are all there at my camp and I can see them in my mind's eye, their faces, their smiles, their laughter. Perhaps there is an immortality to a place, and if so, this might just be the place.

Time is always close by when a river is around, for time and rivers intertwine intrinsically. Without motion there is no time and a river is always in motion. Like people, a river has a beginning, middle, and end. The Deschutes has had a lot of time to move across the landscape: It changed its course from west to north after the Cascades blocked its flow; it sliced through thick lava flows and created a spectacular canyon. Along the way landslides, floods, and earthquakes have altered the river as well. Some ten thousand years ago, a landslide blocked the river above the town of Maupin backing up the river some five miles long and one hundred feet deep. When the dam burst the water sent huge boulders downriver and became Whitehorse Rapids, a Class IV rapid that today still causes boat wrecks and sometimes fatalities, too. Some three thousand years later, a catastrophic flood rearranged the river: Geologists have discovered large river boulders stuck in the dirt some two hundred feet above today's river. I have not heard about the reason behind the flood, but it could be due to an earthquake, volcanic eruption, or a blown-out ice dam. Who knows? The Earth is forever restless.

More recently, Oregon's pioneers began putting their imprint on the Deschutes early on, and the first dam on the river was built in 1922. Called the Crane Prairie Dam, it was some thirteen miles downstream from the river's source. Once used by migratory long-legged cranes, the prairie now lies at the bottom of a large reservoir. Just a little farther downstream of Crane Prairie is another similar dam called Wickiup Dam, which was built in 1949 and was used for irrigation. The earthen dam is two and a half miles long and its reservoir covers an area of seventeen square miles. Like Crane Prairie, it is shallow and the fishing can be quite good. The outlet of Wickup Reservoir is the Deschutes River, and it flows along more like an irrigation ditch than a river there. The unstable flows have largely ruined trout spawning habitat there for miles downstream.

While the river was harnessed on the upper river for irrigation, it was harnessed for hydroelectricity in its middle section. In 1958 Portland General Electric Company (PGE) built Pelton Dam, and just upstream six years later, Round Butte Dam was built. The project provides electricity for an estimated one hundred fifty thousand households. The dams inundated much of the middle Deschutes and the lower ends of its major tributaries, the Crooked River and the Metolius River, and also created a popular boating reservoir called "Lake" Billy Chinook that has three large arms with seventy-two miles of shoreline. I've boated up the reservoir into the arms of all three rivers. I never saw those canyons when those rivers flowed freely, but apparently there was some wonderful fishing there. I do know that anadromous fish such as salmon and steelhead once migrated up those rivers, but the hydroelectric dams blocked those fish runs.

In 2009 PGE built an underwater tower at Round Butte to enable salmon and steelhead to once again utilize those spawning waters above the dams. The new facility ostensibly allows juvenile salmon to swim more safely downstream through the reservoir and down the river back to the ocean. Specifically, the underwater tower allows the dam operator to blend cold and warm waters together and thereby help create a current through the reservoir that, in turn, attracts the juvenile fish to swim to a collection area. There the young fish are trucked around the dams and released in the river. As for the adult salmon, they are trapped at the base of the dam and trucked up into the reservoir where they continue to go up to their spawning waters. It is unclear if the operation has been successful. However, fish conservationists and others have been critical of the new operation, which they claim has resulted in higher water temperatures, poor water quality, reduced aquatic insect populations, more invasive plant and animal species, and, in the end, fewer native trout.

<hr />

Below the dams the river's remaining one hundred miles flow freely from near the town of Madras to the Columbia River. This is the popular area for fly fishermen, rafters, campers, and sightseers. There are few roads in the canyon, so the best way to explore it is by boat. Most of the anglers, rafters, and campers seldom venture far from the bank. Up the slope one hundred feet away from the riparian zone, the vegetation thins out, often into little more than cheatgrass and rock. There are a number of side canyons on either bank of the river, some miles long such as Oak Canyon, Rattlesnake Canyon, and Harris Canyon, but few people venture up into those areas. Up on the top of the canyon's rim are the wheat ranches, some fifteen hundred feet above the banks of the river. The width of the canyon is narrow in some places, but in other areas the rim-to-rim distance is more than ten miles wide. Some call the area between the riverine crowd and the ranchers on top "in-between country." The only people who spend time in this steep, rugged country are cowboys who tend to their cattle and hunters who seek deer, mountain sheep, and chukar partridge in the fall and early winter.

Like most others on the Deschutes, my time has been spent primarily within a few hundred feet of the river's banks. However, I have on occasion ventured into the in-between country to hunt for mule deer and chukar. I have been fortunate to have been "successful" on both counts, but the word *success* is inaccurate for I have thoroughly enjoyed hunting up and down the slopes of the canyon even when I did not come back with any game. I suppose I should have gone into that country just for the fun of it, but for some reason I needed an impetus to hike into that rugged terrain. While not exactly fun, the hard work of chukar hunting was an adventure, and it also was a great way to learn more about the totality of the river's canyon, its essence, rim to rim, not just its watery ribbon and its fish. I am glad I went chukar hunting in that in-between country when I was young, because it is not something you do after your hair turns gray.

I remember one particular hunt quite clearly: It was on a cold January day years ago—back when I had brown hair. I snuggled my wool stocking cap onto my head and assembled my small daypack with water and food, as my friends and I were planning to drop down from the canyon's rim to nearly the bottom of the river, a descent of nearly one thousand feet of elevation. We contoured downward and around the sidehills, following paths worn by cattle and deer when possible, but most of the time blazing new trail in the soil softened by the frost heave and recent snow. On the steeper sections the soil thinned to talus and I had to watch out. Even when careful, I still kicked up small rockslides. On the steepest talus I broke the action of my double-barreled shotgun, uneasy at all the slipping and sliding with a loaded gun in hand.

While we were descending down toward the river bottom, we ran into several feeder canyons. At the mouth of one such canyon, we noticed signs and the dogs noticed that too. For we bipeds, sign means thin green, white-tipped droppings, moist with a freshness indicating that the birds were nearby. For the dogs, sign was in the wind, undetectable with our unsophisticated noses. For us, the world of scent is dimly perceived, black and white at best; for the dogs, it is a Technicolor sensory landscape alive with diversity and meaning. Tom and I pushed the bottom of the draw while Geoff worked the sidehill. More sign.

We silently edged down the dry creek, thick in places with sagebrush tall enough to shade a Sunday picnic. Deer trails wound through the maze, and I only hoped that the birds would not fly at that moment when I could not see beyond the barrels of my gun.

The dogs were out several hundred yards, noses working in the wind, screening out the chukars from the rabbits and meadowlarks. The gully bottom was rocky and the side slopes covered with cheatgrass, leaving few exposed dirt areas to reveal tracks. But the sign—the fresh droppings—were there. There. Again. And again. A chicken coop of sign.

One of Geoff's Brittanies locked onto point—body rigid, frozen, shock still on the hillside above us.

"Up here," whispered Geoff to Tom and me. We puffed up the steep slope, sprinting as fast as we could.

"Here!" Geoff said urgently, as though there should be no problem bounding straight up the steep hillside.

"Just as soon as I get my heart out of my throat," said Tom. And Tom was doing great compared to me. My heart was pounding so hard I could barely see or breathe. My legs had turned to Jell-O. But the dog was still locked up. The air was thick with the tension of the pending flush. We advanced closer, fingering safeties. A dog on point is always a wonderful sight: obedient, purposeful, fulfilling its destiny. We too were fulfilling our destiny, following our predatory instincts that have been honed since the spear and the bow and arrow. While united in our present pursuit, we hunters were on different planes: Geoff was the chukar expert with two devoted Brittanies and a physique developed by spending many hours on the StairMaster. Tom was the big game hunter filling in the down time between the end of elk season and the spring turkey opener. I was the fly-fishing guy filling in the down time before the spring hatches on the Deschutes.

The canyon was absolutely still, not a sound save my labored breathing that condensed in the cold air. The explosion of birds always takes you by surprise, even when you are ready for it. Suddenly, more than a dozen ghost-gray forms burst from the thin cover and rocketed down the slope.

Incoming at eleven o'clock. We all fired. No hits. Surprisingly for Geoff and Tom. Not me. My shot was hopelessly behind, confounded once again by the downslope angle. The dog looked puzzled, looked for the retrieve that was not to be. I saw the birds in my mind over and over: gliding with wings set, down, down, down into the void below the vast chasm of space between us and the river. Like other upland birds, chukars flush with an explosion of wingbeats that quickly cease . . . and then they glide. The difference between chukars and other upland birds is that they inhabit steep terrain and nearly always flush downhill, so once off the ground and airborne, they glide forever. They are never close for more than an instant. They rocket off, set their wings, and slowly their dark little shapes—like small shadows racing across the sage—melt into the ocean of air below.

Later, after working the feeder canyon, we continued hunting down the slope, Tom and Geoff fanning across the side-slope. I was snaking my way down the crotch of a gully, threading along faint game trails through the wild rose and pungent sage. Out in the distance the blue of the Deschutes was a contrast to the brown-gray landscape. Thick electric cables draped between large transmission towers that marched across the canyon. When I got near them, I could hear the hum of hydroelectricity, wheeling from Grand Coulee Dam to Bakersfield, from McNary Dam to Sacramento.

I heard a gunshot on the slope above me. It was probably Geoff centering yet another unlucky chukar in the middle of his 20-gauge pattern. Suddenly, a singleton flushed and startled me with its flurry. Put your lips together and blow: That is the sound of a chukar's wings beating furiously, propelling it downhill like a bullet. But the bird held tight and flushed close, and despite my initial surprise I was able to swing on it, pull the trigger, and the bird hit the bottom of the rocky gully hard. By the time I found it, the death twitches had subsided and I picked up the black-masked, red-beaked bird, its plumpness and soft-feathered body comforting to my cold, wind-dried hands. Then I stuffed it into the game pouch of my hunting vest.

Up close, chukars are surprisingly colorful, their gray-toned bodies alive with dark bars on their flanks, tan and blue hues on their breast and back, and red legs. On the flush they usually offer little more than a blur of blue-gray to shoot at, except for the times when you are real close and you can see the distinctive black mask that runs across their eyes and down across their throats. Native to central Asia, this member of the partridge family has firmly established itself into the West's most inhospitable country, the eroded canyons and badlands where few other animals—including humans—survive. Smaller than pheasants and larger than quail, chukars have adapted well, apparently displacing nothing native and rewarding us in return.

We dropped down nearly to the bottom of the canyon, and the terrain there was not as steep and more hospitable: level land, running water, vegetation—as a people, we are more comfortable with such things. Rock cliffs, waterless talus slopes, scant vegetation—we are uncomfortable with terrain like that, in-between country. We nooned there about a quarter of a mile upslope from the river, ate our sandwiches, drank our water, and as the weather was still cold, we made a small warming fire down in a little hollow with some scraps of newspaper and dead sagebrush. The wispy flames felt wonderful up against our backsides. The flames and orange glowing embers seemed so civilized in this lonely, harsh land. Geoff uncapped his water bottle and gave some of it to the dogs. They were tired but still excited, ready to find birds. I was ready for some more birds, too, but I groaned inwardly when I looked up at the top of the rim that I would have to climb back up before dark. I wished that there was a ski chair-lift handy.

Slowly, we trudged up from the river, watching the dogs zigzag across the slope, sniffing as the wind shifted about, poking into brushy patches and across the thin carpet of cheatgrass. From a distance the undulating hillsides looked like naked thighs, crisscrossed, one lapping across the other, folding into the draws and coulees that stretch out across the canyon. Every now and again I looked down at the river itself, a view that most people seldom see, a view where the river appears placid, the riffles just little white curls on the blue water, the rapids mute, as quiet as the silent towering basalt cliffs. The winter light weakened and before long, in the pre-dark cooling, came the fog, rolling down from the rim, shapeless, omnipresent, obscuring the transmission towers that serve as reference points. The fog appears to be out of character in this open country where you can see for miles in every direction. But in the winter, fog is not uncommon. It softens this rocky, jagged land with a heavy dampness that is both soothing and claustrophobic.

The push up the final slope was murder—a reminder that time never rests and the body ages all too fast and all too certainly. My lungs could not absorb enough oxygen, and my knees could hardly lift my feet. My boots felt that they each weighed twenty pounds, not two. I gingerly walked around a brickbat basalt formation and then entered into a stand of scrub oaks. I glanced up. A porcupine was in the branches, its primitive, hunkered body immobile but watchful of the weary hunters. Above the porcupine drifted the fog. In a minute I was out of the trees and ran into the fog like a gray wall. Like a snowstorm that fuses sky to earth with a blank whiteness, so this fog had fused the gray sky to the gray-brown chukar earth. Fog may come in on little cat's feet, but once it arrives it settles in like an elephant, dominating the landscape, obscuring all worldly reference points beyond the next clump of bunch grass.

Out up in the distance, I heard Geoff and Tom talking. Then I heard the dog whistle. I no longer heard any telltale "chuck, chuck, chuck" clucking of the birds in the distance as we did earlier in the day, for it was too dark and the birds were settled down for the night. I marked the dog whistle and took an aural compass reading. A flushed chukar would disappear into the murk in an instant. The sun had set and the brief winter twilight was over before it started, the stars and the moon hidden by the fog. The ground continued to flatten and before long I found the fence line that would lead to the car.

The headlights of the car cut through the fog as we drove toward the highway. Down below the canyon's rim, the fog continued to flow down the draws like a headless ghost, covering our footprints, moistening the sage and grass and rocks. And in the cold of the new morning, the white of frost would be hard on the land, top to bottom, rim to rim.

Rim to rim, headwaters to confluence, tributary upon tributary, the Deschutes would continue to flow to the sea throughout the winter, in places the river's edge brittle with ice around the dark-colored boulders, the banks white with snow. Up in the Cascades, not far from Little Lava Lake, the snow would cover the duff and rocky soil. A few months later the snow would begin to melt, the water trickling down into the sponge of the lava beds, the water coursing its way down through hidden cracks and tunnels and hollows . . . and ready to work its way back up, too, to percolate up toward the surface again someday, sometime, ready to be a river again.

CHAPTER THREE

Caldera Headwaters

THE HEADWATERS OF OREGON'S DESCHUTES RIVER LIE PRIMARILY west of the river, in the foothills of the Cascade Range. But the upper Deschutes includes some headwaters to the east as well, such as Paulina Lake and nearby East Lake, which flow into Paulina Creek and, in turn, into the Deschutes. What is distinctive about these two lakes is that they are not only good fishing lakes, but that they lie in the caldera of an active volcano, which has been designated as the Newberry National Volcanic Monument. Unlike the cone-shaped Cascade volcanoes of Mount Adams and Mount Rainier, Newberry is a shield volcano with some four hundred volcanic vents. The apron of the lava that flowed across those vents covers an area the size of Rhode Island and is the largest volcano in the Cascade Range.

The bubbling magma under Newberry Volcano has leaked out over four hundred thousand years, and seventy-five thousand years ago, the volcano exploded violently leaving volcanic ash deposits as far away as the San Francisco Bay. The overlying rocks collapsed when the magma chamber emptied and created a massive depression, what geologists call a caldera. The Newberry caldera itself encompasses seventeen square miles, including the two lakes. The explosion also sliced off the volcano's peak by as much as one thousand feet. Today the summit of the volcano is called Paulina Peak at an elevation of 7,984 feet.

The most recent Newberry eruption was during the Middle Ages, about the time of Charlemagne in the land of the Franks. The only humans in the Pacific Northwest who witnessed the eruption were some

Indian tribes who frequented the caldera in the summer. The base of the caldera has an elevation of sixty-four hundred feet, so it is too cold for human habitation year-round. Of course, we do not know how far away the Indians were when Newberry erupted: If they were close by, they were likely killed. The eruption caused explosive plumes of volcanic ash and pyroclastic flows. Rocks and ash fell into the caldera ten feet deep; airborne ash drifted as far as eastern Idaho. Some of the lava flows turned into a huge field of obsidian. Shiny and glossy black, this volcanic glass can be shaped into a knife edge as sharp as Solingen steel. Before long the Indians discovered this new find and Newberry obsidian was traded widely around the West over the centuries.

Both of the lakes are as serene as a lake can be, but that is deceptive because under the surface just a mile or two below the bottom of the two lakes lies molten rock, magma. Hot as blazes, deep inside the Earth, this heat creates hot springs that, in turn, seep into the lakes and those waters bring up minerals and gases that utilize various life forms. Newberry is an active volcano and as the US Geological Survey says: "Newberry volcano is certain to erupt again." With the city of Bend twenty miles away, geologists closely monitor the volcano with seismometers stationed around the caldera. The instruments can detect and measure the swelling and contractions of the volcano, the beating of the mountain's heart, its vast reservoir of magma churning, splashing, red-hot like a medieval painting of Hell.

Of the thousands of lakes in the West, there are few that lie in the belly of a volcano. And surprisingly, those twin lakes are not only scenic but they also are good for fishing. Oregon's largest brown trout was caught at Paulina Lake in 2002 weighing in at twenty-eight pounds. At East Lake the record brown trout is a twenty-two-pounder displayed at the resort's Blue Duck Grill. Rainbow trout have been caught up to twelve pounds. Introduced landlocked sockeye salmon and landlocked Atlantic salmon also thrive in those lakes due to the cold, clear water and rich nutrients.

East Lake, where I fish most of the time, is a deep lake with a depth of 170 feet, and it is about two miles across. Generally, deep lakes are not especially good for fishing, especially fly fishing, because sunlight, and life itself, begins to vanish when the water gets too deep. Plus, fly lines are not generally effective below thirty feet deep. Casting any fly line that would work deeper than that would be the antithesis of fly fishing, or so it seems to me. To fish any deeper you might as well put your fly rod away and grab a level-wind outfit—and maybe you should use a downrigger, as well. While the middle of East Lake is deep, it has extensive shallows and aquatic vegetation, and that is what makes fly fishing good there. Aquatic vegetation—what we usually call weeds—provides the habitat, and that, in turn, enables millions of aquatic insects, such as midges, mayflies, and damselflies, to live and reproduce there. And likewise, forage fish and leeches add to the fish's ample menu.

While the waters in the two lakes have been rich for millennia, fish arrived only recently. Early in the twentieth century, scientists traveled to the lakes and determined that they were devoid of fish. Scientists say that millions of years ago fish colonized the waters of the Deschutes River and upstream into Paulina Creek, the outlet of the lakes. But the fish could not get over Paulina Creek Falls. Apparently, crayfish were able to crawl their way up the rocks over the falls, move upstream through the creek, and enter the lakes. But fish do not have the wherewithal to climb rocks, and so the fish remained down in the creek below the falls. Such is the case in a number of other high-elevation western mountain lakes devoid of fish where waterfalls have blocked fish colonization.

From the angler's point of view, human intervention has been a blessing. In 1912 a group of Bend-area citizens toted canisters of water and trout fingerlings onto buckboards and drove them up the slopes of the Newberry caldera. Where the wagon road ended, the pioneers hoisted the canisters onto mules and ferried the mule trains to the shores of the lakes where they released the fish. The fish did well, but like many other high-elevation mountain lakes, there are few inlet creeks that provide adequate spawning areas. As a result, in those lakes—such as East Lake and Paulina Lake—an ongoing fishery requires regular hatchery releases.

The headwaters of a river like the Deschutes include not only the alpine creeks, springs, and streams, but mountain lakes, as well. Both East Lake and Paulina Lake are headwater lakes. East Lake has no visible outlet; its waters seep out underground and flow into Paulina Lake. That lake, in turn, has a visible outlet, and it is called Paulina Creek, where it flows westward into the upper Deschutes. Actually, there are a number of lakes that do not have a visible outlet, including Crater Lake, the nation's deepest lake. Every year an average of sixty-six inches of rain and forty feet of snow is recorded at Crater Lake. Somehow that rain and melted snow does not fill up the crater and spill out over the rim. The lake maintains its current level because the amount of rain and snowfall equals the evaporation and seepage rate.

All lakes entail evaporation, though at East Lake there is not much evaporation going on during the cold months because evaporation is an endothermic process that entails the addition of heat to accomplish. In their liquid form water molecules are always moving, but the sun's heat causes those molecules to move about more rapidly. Occasionally, a molecule breaks the bonds linking it to other water molecules and it flies off into the air. It has been vaporized. It is still water, but it is now in a gaseous state. The warmer the temperature, the more rapidly the molecules move and the more often they break free of their bonds. The energy used to evaporate water becomes locked up in the water molecules as they turn from a liquid to a gas. This latent energy will be released later when the air cools and the gas condenses back into liquid water as rain droplets.

Between atmospheric evaporation and inlet and outlet creeks, a lake is forever recirculated and made afresh over and over. On the surface it appears that rivers connote movement and lakes connote stillness, but that is not true. The word *stillwater* is really a misnomer because lakes are seldom still. Lakes are an integral part of a river basin that comprises a network of rills, creeks, streams, ponds, lakes, and rivers that flow to the sea. A river's current obviously has movement, but lakes also have their own movement; it is just more subtle. In shallow lakes the movement of the wind circulates the water back and forth. Deeper lakes have thermal-driven movement, as well. Waters in such lakes have different temperatures, and those temperatures have different densities. As the seasons change, the warming and cooling layers of waters in the lake create different densities and consequently those layers intermix. That intermixing enables nutrients to rise from the bottom to the top and make them available to plants and animals.

Nearly every time that I have strung up my six-weight lake fly rod and headed out to a body of "still" water, I have found that wind has been my constant companion. Once upon a time I had thought maybe it was just me, but that is not so. I eventually realized that wind is the result of differences in air temperatures and air pressure. For example, on a summer day on a typical lake in the mountains, the surrounding land heats up, and the warm air rises leaving behind low pressure near the ground. Cool marine air is trapped above the lake's surface, and that colder air has more pressure than does warm air. Nature abhors a vacuum, so on a warm summer day, that colder high-pressure air above the lake rushes in to equalize the low pressure near the surrounding land of the lake. The result is wind. Such winds are more common in the summer where there is a greater difference between the cool marine air above the lake and the warming adjoining land. Such winds also are often most common in the afternoon, after the land heats up. After sunset the land cools and commensurately the wind often dissipates quickly.

To the fly angler, that means that the mornings and evenings will often have less wind than in the afternoon. I have experienced this a number of times, and often in the early evening, I have waited to get out on the water until the wind finally abates. At other times I have gotten impatient and gone out fishing in spite of the wind—just hoping that it would stop. While bothersome, wind is after all what animates the waters and lands of the Earth, for a windless world bereft of rippling waters and rustling leaves would be a somnolent world. On a lake, for example, a wind can energize baitfish and bugs, plus a bit of chop on a lake's surface decreases visibility, thereby making the fish less nervous and that, in turn, helps the angler.

While lakes and rivers both entail movement, nonetheless they differ greatly. Lakes are like mesas—a horizontal landscape—their gradient nonexistent. Rivers by contrast are vertical as they flow ever downward in elevation, cutting their ways through canyons and valleys. Also, rivers talk: Eddies gurgle, rapids roar, and riffles chatter. A river is very vocal. While a lake is certainly alive, it is mute. It says nothing. It is quieter than the ocean, for a lake has little or no surf, save the wind-blown whitecaps that crash onto the beach. A becalmed lake is so quiet you can hear voices across the water hundreds of yards away. A lake at night is especially quiet, as quiet as quiet can be, even more quiet than a deep wood because tree branches and nocturnal animals rustle about in the darkest of places. Out in a boat on a lake, there is nothing else around to rustle. The space around the shoreline is wide open, filled with nothing more than invisible gases, airborne pollens, and dust. There is nothing there to rustle about on a windless piece of open water; it is as though sound no longer exists.

I remember at Miller Lake one time—a remote lake south and west of East Lake—I walked down from camp in the evening and jumped into my drift boat. I rowed out several hundred yards into the blackness of the night to try to fish for the big nocturnal piscivorous brown trout that I had been hearing about. The sun had long since set and the moon was AWOL. I dipped the oars into the dark water but could not see the oar blades. They disappeared into the blackness. I took another stroke and had to feel where the blades touched the water. All I could see was an unnerving blackness where the water and air melded into a lonely one-ness. I did not know the viscosity of the blackness, whether it was thick or thin, whether or not the oar blades struck air or water. I looked above and the stars were strewn about as they do, sparkling but distant. My ears were ringing. I turned on my headlamp for a minute or two and unfurled my rod and cast out onto the water. Then I clicked the light off to avoid spooking any cruising fish. I could hear the slap of the water on the line and then it disappeared. The line sank down a few feet and then I slowly retrieved my streamer fly. And then again and again.

After twenty minutes or so I gave up. With so little light it was difficult to cast. The world was deathly quiet, no boats were on the water, just some distant orange flames of a campfire on the shore of the campground. I do not know what I would have done if I had hooked one of those large browns. It would have been a god-awful tangle of leader and line and oars and net and rod and who knows what else. I reeled in the line the best I could and laid the rod down. I took hold of the oars, and with the flickering pinpoint of the campfire as a target, I rowed back to camp. The only sounds I heard were the oars creaking in the oar locks and the water dripping off the oar blades as they came out of the water.

Like Miller Lake, fish behave differently in a lake than they do in a river. In a river the fish station themselves in feeding lanes; the biggest ones get the best spots. The fish's food is a moveable feast: The insects, some alive and others dead, flow downriver with the current. The trout examine the morsels as they go by and then attack them or ignore them. In contrast, on a lake there is no current so the fish cruise around looking for prey.

Early on, most fly anglers recognize good fishing spots on streams and rivers, such as riffles, back eddies, structure, edges, foam lines, and runs. A river's actual surface water area is limited. When you are wading in a river, you look up and down the river only a hundred yards or so either way, and the total surface area may measure only a few hundred square yards at best. In contrast, a lake's surface area is measured in acres or square miles. On East Lake the far shore is two miles wide. With all that water, where in the world should the angler go?

First of all, not all lakes are equal. Clean water is an essential ingredient to a good fishing lake, but the waters of some lakes, such as Crater Lake and Waldo Lake in Oregon's Cascades, are so pure that the fishing is poor due to the lack of nutrients and plant growth. The spectacular deep-blue color of Crater Lake is a wonder to tourists but not so terrific for anglers. A good fishing lake should have more of a greenish tinge to it, because the suspended organic matter helps better absorb light and promote more plant growth.

A good fishing lake should have shallows, because that is where the aquatic plants live and plant growth is essential to fish survival. Some plants, such as water milfoils, are rooted at the bottom. Other plants, such as lily pads, float on the water. Aquatic plants are the building blocks of life in a lake: The zooplankton and tiny animal organisms feed on the plants; in turn, insects and leeches feed on those smaller organisms; and likewise the trout eat the insects and leeches. The edges between the light-colored shallows and the deeper darker-colored water can be especially promising. Generally, a good fishing lake has a weedy or rocky bottom; a sandy or muddy bottom is not usually productive. Shoals are sunken islands, and like shallows, they are a lighter color than the surrounding deep water. Fortunately, nearly all lakes have wind (sometimes too much!) and wind is critical for fish survival. Insects fall into a lake every day and those dead and nearly dead insects drift toward the shore.

As for the actual act of lake fishing, as a boy I used a Mitchell 300 spinning reel and an Eagle Claw rod using everything from Pautzke's Balls of Fire to wedding rings to rooster tails. While a fly angler now for many decades, I still tie on a certain dead-ringer lure instead of a fly when I get frustrated and absolutely nothing else works—when the Woolly Buggers don't work, when the *Callibaetis* emergers fail, when the midges fail, and when the inch-long-and-green damselfly nymphs fail. From my boyhood days on, I have relied on a small Flatfish, whether it is attached to a spinning rod or a fly rod—it does not matter. In the old days such lures were labeled as Fly Rod Flatfish for they were small enough and light enough to still easily cast with fly gear. So every few years when nothing else works on a lake, I have resorted to crimping a small split-shot on the leader about a foot or two above a small Flatfish and then trolling slowly around the perimeter of the lake. When that does not titillate the fish, then nothing will, so you might as well head back to the shore. Since the first Flatfish was sold, its wobbling action, especially in trolling, has been irresistible to predator fish. Tens of millions of Flatfish have been sold over the years, and its inventor, Charlie Helin, an autoworker in Detroit, became a rich man since he patented the lure in 1936. First made of wood and later plastic, the built-in diving lip quickly gets the lure down into the strike zone. Moreover, it has a wobbling, side-to-side motion that is effective regardless of the speed of the retrieve. I have tried to design a fly that replicates the movement of a Flatfish, but as yet I have not found one.

As effective as they are, the few Flatfish in my tackle box lie fallow, for I prefer to fish with flies and not lures. Consequently, my fly boxes are stuffed with all manner of flies from tiny midges to large streamers. As a fly angler, I pay close attention to what the fish eat. I have found that generally the array of prey in a lake is more limited than that in moving water. In a lake such prey include leeches, forage fish, crustaceans like crayfish, and several aquatic insects, mostly midges, damselflies, dragonflies, *Callibaetis*, and a smattering of caddisflies. To be sure there are other items on a lake trout's menu, but those are the major ones.

One of the most prolific insect hatches on western lakes is the *Calli-baetis* mayfly. For some reason the weed beds in East Lake seem to prop-agate a large number of those mayflies. I have seen them in the air by the thousands, hovering, drifting with the wind, instinctively "thinking" about where and when to mate and later when to drop their eggs onto the water. And shortly thereafter they die—but most likely they do not know that.

At any rate, after the *Callibaetis*' eggs hatch out down at the bottom of the lake, these medium-sized, tan and grayish nymphs feed on the algae that attach to various aquatic plants. Within less than two months of their birth, those slender nymphs mature, form wing pads, and swim up to the surface where they shed their exoskeleton and emerge as dainty, winged mayflies. The process of swimming from the bottom of the lake to the surface takes time. And on the surface it takes time for the bug to wiggle out of its outer garment. During all that time there is plenty of time for a bug to be eaten by a waiting trout. And for a lot of *Callibaetis*, that is exactly what happens.

For any aquatic insect it must be an epic journey to swim its way through the fish-infested waters and finally reach the surface, ready to transform itself from a creature of the water to one of the air. The meta-morphosed mayfly discards its gills apparatus and begins to breathe the oxygen of the air. It flexes its six skinny legs and then it checks out its new wings—those lovely, molted, veined wings, like tiny sails. It has broken through the surface of the water, a huge effort for a bug, and it is on the surface, like liquid glass, warming itself in the midday sun. It is there, in the ready room, ready to spread it wings . . . ready to fly at last . . . and then . . . then . . . just before takeoff . . . gulp . . . down the hatch.

Maybe the *Callibaetis* got chewed up in the fish's sharp teeth and died instantly. Or maybe it was swallowed whole and worked its way through the fish's digestive tract to finally be smothered in the fish's dark stomach, an ignominious death, indeed. I have cleaned many fish and often dissected the stomach contents to ascertain what the fish were taking. By the time the bugs are actually in the fish's stomach, they are as dead as a door nail; however, I have sliced open a trout's upper gullet and found it stuffed with whole, wiggling bugs. Nature is not a tidy place wherein to die.

From the trout's point of view, it looks upward at little wiggly things on the surface of the lake, ready to slap at the genuine article. Genuine is the key word, because the trout, at least at East Lake, are fussy, maybe because they are heavily fished during the summer months. Who knows? In a river the bugs slide by quickly with the current, and the fish have to take it quickly if they want it at all. But in a lake the trout have plenty of time to examine the bugs while they rise to the surface, be they *Callibaetis* or midges or maybe caddis pupae. Trout are good at checking out their dinner fare. They seem to instinctively know that by eating a counterfeit morsel they may end up on the wrong end of a line, a line that is attached to a giant creature, grinning, clumsy, and ready to kill. So they look closely at the bug's shape, size, color, and its action. If something is off, just a bit, the fish more than likely will beg off.

To the fly angler, this can be exasperating. I remember one time recently at East Lake when my boat had been anchored in about eight feet of water, right along the edge of the weeds. It was late morning and a hatch of *Callibaetis* was going on, not a blizzard, but clearly the bugs were hatching and hovering about as mayflies do. There were rises here and there around the boat. I looked at my fly box and thought about tying on a standard adult *Callibaetis*, such as a Comparadun. Or maybe I should tie on an emerger, like a Quigley Cripple, an imitation whereby the fly awkwardly tries to escape its nymphal shuck near the surface. Earlier in the year I had tied up a variation of just such a pattern. It had a body of pheasant tail fibers ribbed with thin gold wire and some grizzly hackle. Near the front of the hook, I tied on a stack of deer hair, facing out beyond the eye of the hook.

So, I tied on the cripple, though it took some time to put the 5X tippet through the deer hair that was hard up against the eye of the hook. At last I dabbed some floatant on the tip of the deer hairs. The idea was to cast out the fly onto the water and have the fly dangle vertically just below the surface with only the top deer hairs floating in the air. I cast a cripple out and then I let it alone. While there was no current, there was a breeze and the fly line floated along just as though there was a slow current. I had to manage the floating line so it would not tangle as the fly moved toward the boat with the wind. The leader was long and I wanted there to be no drag, but at the same time I wanted the line to be reasonably straight in case the fish struck.

It did not take long, and a fine rainbow hit the cripple and it fought well. Later I caught another nice fish. However, the next time I saw a splash at the end of my line, I found only a rejection. And then again. And again.

I moved some fifty feet away and re-anchored. While the water was still alive with rises, I found only rejections. Fly anglers call this a rise refusal. I finally took off the cripple and tied on a standard adult, heavily hackled and well lubricated with floatant so the fly would float right on the surface. No luck. A trout would rise at the fly, slap it, make a swirl on the water . . . but no cigar.

What was going on?

I noticed that the wind had died down and that was not good: A bit of ripple on the surface is always good as that helps to camouflage the fish underneath. On a clear glassy surface, the fish can see right through the water column compared to the surface with a wind chop. Or maybe I was casting too much. I know that on a lake you are supposed to cast and let the fly stay put: Let the fish go to the fly, not the other way around as you would on a river. Or maybe I should have targeted the fish at an angle away from the previous rise and not directly at the rise. Maybe I should have tied on a smaller fly. Or maybe I should have snipped off the tippet and tied on a blood knot with an even finer tippet. Maybe I had too much slack line on the water. Maybe I needed a longer leader. Maybe I should have sat down in the boat to cast rather than cast standing up, because a six-foot vertical shape on a lake's surface can be a warning signal to the fish that something is amiss. Maybe. Maybe.

The only sure thing I knew was that those fish rejected the fly on purpose, not because they had missed the fly. If they had wanted to eat the fly, they would have known how to do it. Trout have lightning speed, agile movements, and a maw large enough to devour prey from midges to mice.

I picked up the anchor, cranked up the trolling motor, and headed back to the other side of the lake. The flatness of the hull slapped at the chop, the air rushing by my face, the sun warmer by the minute, and I recalled what an old-time fly fisherman once told me: "Behind every rejection, there's usually a message."

At camp I mulled over what that message might be, and even into the depths of the cold night, when I tossed back and forth in my sleeping bag, I was at a loss. Finally, I said to myself: "It's just fishing." Sometimes you have to tell yourself that. That is why fishing—whatever it is called—is so wonderful. Is it a sport? Maybe . . . but it is not like bowling or golf or baseball. There are no bleachers, no spectators, no rules, no winners, no losers, no score, and no prizes. The point of fishing is simply to outwit the wily trout: It is more than a sport, for sure. And yet, even a fly-fishing guide friend of mine once told me: "It's just fishing." You cannot say that about open-heart surgery: "Oh, it's just surgery." The consequence of one is life and death and the other is that sometimes you do not get the jolt that you wanted at the end of the line. I do not expect to catch fish. Fishing is one thing; catching is another. I am always excited before I get on the fishing waters, but I do not expect or assume that the fish will accommodate my wishes. There are times when the fish put superglue on their lips. There are times when they bite at most anything from marshmallows to bare hooks. But it is the times in between that you need to focus on. An effective angler needs knowledge and experience. But beyond that an angler needs two additional indispensable ingredients: hope and luck.

What is hope?

Hope is a mix of expectation and desire. And luck . . . well . . . luck is the second cousin of fate, as fickle and unpredictable as the wind. You do not have to be lucky, but you have to believe in luck, because sometimes skill is not enough.

The next day my friend Vance came into camp, and later in the afternoon we took the boat out onto the lake planning to use some midge patterns because a couple of other anglers had done quite well on zebra midges earlier in the day. We anchored up alongside of some high cliffs. We played out the anchor rope and determined that the depth was about ten feet. We used a long leader and put a strike indicator on the leader about nine feet above the fly. We put a split-shot on the tippet and put the whole assemblage overboard. The idea was that the fly would be suspended about a foot off the bottom. I have been told that in most lakes midges are omnipresent and most of the time they hover near the bottom of the lake. And where there is prey, there will be fish.

We waited for our strike indicator to bob up and down on the surface, and sure enough before long we were not disappointed. Often, the strikes did not result in hooking a fish, but a few did and we got the fish boated. That evening we were indeed lucky and landed several nice fish. I caught my first landlocked sockeye salmon, called kokanee. It was about fourteen inches long and quite a fighter. The other fish were rainbows. While earlier in the day, the wind had made fishing challenging, as the sun started to set, the wind died, as it often does in the evening on summer days high in the mountains. The ripples across the water had become almost glass-like, the shimmering light slowly fading, the air cooling. Before long I had to put on my jacket against the cold.

Suddenly, Vance and I noticed some bubbling and swirling water not far from the boat. We were surprised at the activity on the lake for it was otherwise placid. Bubble, bubble, toil and trouble. Like a witch's brew, the troubled water bubbled away and suddenly a mat of green plants about three feet in diameter popped out of the depths.

Wow!

"What's going on?" asked Vance.

I certainly did not have the answer. The water continued to boil and another patch of green plants appeared. The mat of plants was a light-colored green, low on the water and floating with no apparent effort. We were puzzled. Somehow it gave me the creeps. I had been told that there were volcanic vents and hot springs at the bottom of the lake. I guess we found one.

It was unnerving to me that we were floating on a lake in a crater of an active volcano. I thought of the early Earth, when it was brand new, nothing but an amalgamation of hot rocks, and how over time the planet cooled down and how the moisture in the rocks began to de-gas and released water vapor into the air. Eventually, the vapor condensed into droplets and they, in turn, grew larger and heavier and formed raindrops and those raindrops fell out of the sky for centuries upon centuries and the deluge covered the Earth with a worldwide ocean, only tiny bits of land poking out of the lifeless water. There were no rivers then for there was no land. Tectonic forces were at work in the interior, fueled by radioactive heating of the inner core, and those uplifting forces and volcanism eventually buckled the Earth's crust and formed continents. Before long the first single-cell life forms appeared, most likely in shallow bays and seas and in the deep-sea volcanic vents where heat and gases bubbled up through the crust. Those single-cell organisms multiplied into a dizzy array of life forms, and after a few million years, we ended up with two men in a boat. And nearby them was a little mat of green lying upon the face of the waters, masking the primordial activity below, the volcanic vents and springs in the bottom of the lake bubbling and hissing into the lake's cold water, fueled by subaqueous molten magma. Here was life from bottom to top, turning magma into plants, creating water out of land.

Vance and I looked at one another.

"Weird," is all I could say. Then overhead a pair of mallards circled around our boat and landed on the mat of green. I looked at Vance again.

"Hello?"

The ducks paddled about as ducks do, the drake handsome with its green-colored head, the hen a bit plain save a white-trimmed purple patch on each wing. The ducks appeared to be eating either the plants themselves or the insects that were on the plants. Or maybe both. Then half a dozen more mallards came out of nowhere and descended onto the tiny newborn island.

"Let's get out of here," I said. For some reason I did not want my small zebra midge dangling around in a water world of mysterious gases, springs, and newly sown plants. Plus, I did not want to try to fish near a flock of swimming ducks. I reeled up the fly and slipped it into the keeper. Then I pulled up the anchor and cranked up the outboard.

"*Vámanos!*" I said as I pushed the lever on the side of the engine into forward gear. Then I twisted my hand on the handle of the tiller and turned up the gas. The boat turned around and sped away. I looked back and saw that the ducks were still busy eating whatever they had discovered.

As we moved along through the water, I looked over at the western horizon; the dark green coniferous forest was already asleep, shadowlands tucked away into the draws and gullies, the undulating slopes flattened with the fading light. At this high elevation, the sky was broad and deep. Smoke from a distant forest fire had drifted into the area, so soot and dust thickened the atmospheric soup and inflamed the slanted dying sunlight. Above the caldera's rim was a blood red sky, the sun trying to break through the haze before it disappeared another day, a day unlike any other for every day is a special day, my day, your day, a day like no other, filled with a million things to do and see . . . and . . . unfortunately . . . one less day . . . one less day than the allotment of days that we have. Meanwhile, the lake's darkening sheen seemed timeless, its allotment of days forever, its timeline unfathomable to us, its waters filled to the brim nestled into the pocket of the caldera.

As I piloted the boat toward shore, I stared into the dimness trying to find the right anchoring spot along the beach . . . that big rock over next to the driftwood snag . . . yes, that one. Almost no one was on the beach now and the campers were sitting around their cozy campfires. I shut off the engine, tilting the outboard up so the propeller would not dig into the muddy bottom of the shallow water. The boat coasted onto the beach. I stepped out of the boat and looked back at the lake and the overhead lights had started to turn on, first the evening star, barely visible through the haze but still there, Venus, our next door neighbor. A crescent moon appeared, its curvature as graceful as the muted sunset, its ghostly, splotchy whiteness cratered, its atmosphere nonexistent, defenseless against incomers hurling through space, smashing into that lunar surface, dust flying all over. And back down at the lake, I looked out toward the far shore where some of that 1,044-acre lake will seep through the cracks at the bottom of the lake, downward into its twin and its outlet creek, which will trickle down the slope of the volcano, its ponderosa pine landscape flattening out toward the confluence of another river where, in turn, it will flow downhill serpentine-like, its rapids roaring like a lion, its waters flowing all the way to the River of the West and into the Big Salt. It will be a long journey from the calm waters of the lake nestled in the caldera all the way down to the mouth of the Columbia where it will meet the boisterous tides, its ebbs and flows, timeless, energized by a lifeless orb far away.

It was all more than I could comprehend, so Vance and I grabbed our rods and gear and picked our way along a trail that would go back to camp through a thicket of trees, screened from the lake's winds, comfortable with the tents and cots and comfortable, too, knowing that another day had been well spent. As an old Roman named Seneca once said on the shortness of life: "Life is long if you know how to use it."

Chapter Four

Of Quicksand and Rainbows

On March 29, 1932, the US Corps of Engineers and the Federal Power Commission presented a plan to Congress for building a number of dams for "improving the Columbia River and minor tributaries for the purpose of navigation and efficient development of water-power, and control of floods and the needs of irrigation." The plan soon became a reality, and from the Depression days into the late 1970s, the dam builders went to work. Eventually, more than four hundred dams were built on the Columbia River and its tributaries, some large mainstem dams and others smaller dams on the tributaries. Most noteworthy, hydroelectricity was inexpensive to generate, compared to using other types of power, and the Columbia had plenty of running water: All we had to do was to block the river, raise the water level, impound it, and then let gravity go to work as the water flowed through the penstocks and twirled the turbine blades around and around thereby generating electricity. Plus, with the impoundments there was ample irrigation water, as well, so the interior Northwest could cultivate something other than sagebrush.

The Columbia and its largest tributary, the Snake River, found themselves drastically altered by the dams—from Bonneville to Wanapam, from Ice Harbor to Hells Canyon, from Grand Coulee to Mica. As a youth living on the middle section of the Columbia, I witnessed dam after dam being built on the Columbia and Snake Rivers. It was not until I was much older that I realized the impact of the dams on the salmon and the river itself. More than half of the spawning and rearing habitat once available to salmon and steelhead in the Columbia basin was blocked by the dams. Some other dams had fish ladders so anadromous fish could go upriver to their remaining spawning grounds. However, migrating juvenile fish traveling downriver to the ocean were not always able to find the fish ladders, so some of them ended up getting sucked into the intakes of the powerhouses where they were killed by the thousands by turbine blades measuring twelve feet across and weighing twenty thousand pounds each. The whirling blades create tremendous water pressure that can peel bits of steel off the underside blades in a process called cavitation. And as a boy, I was not the only one who did not realize the impact of the dams on the salmon. In 1946 Frank Bell, vice president of the Columbia River Development League and former US Commissioner of Fisheries, said turbine passage at Bonneville Dam appeared only to leave juvenile fish "groggy."

By the early 1990s the Columbia River salmon and steelhead runs were beginning to be listed under the federal Endangered Species Act. In one of the most bountiful salmon rivers in the world, the salmon and steelhead runs were headed toward extinction. By then most of the basin was pretty well filled up with dams; in fact, the pendulum began to swing in the opposite direction. Eventually, some small dams began to be demolished, usually because of the deleterious effects on migrating salmon. One of those Columbia River tributaries, the Sandy River, had a private utility-owned dam named Marmot Dam upriver some thirty miles from the confluence of the Columbia. It was not a large dam, only forty-seven feet high, but it nonetheless generated electricity beginning in 1913. As in many other places, even small dams can imperil salmon runs and the Sandy was not alone.

In 2007 I was living in Portland and was able to witness the removal of Marmot Dam. It was not especially dramatic. In an odd way the destruction of Marmot Dam saddened me a bit with the environmentalists cheering as the first dynamite blast echoed across the narrow gorge. I talked to one of the engineers watching the event and he shook his head, saying how strange it was that an inexpensive, clean, sustainable source of power was being blown to smithereens. The heavy equipment punctured the dam and the water slowly leaked out through the broken concrete slabs. Week by week the demolition crew removed the chunks of concrete. Before too long the debris was hauled away and the river unloosened itself, like a snake that had been coiled up in a cage and now was slithering freely.

Strangely, the Sandy had a similar situation some two hundred years earlier. Then it was blocked by sand and debris—not concrete and rebar. Eventually, it unloosened itself too, without the use of dynamite, and flowed down the slopes of Mount Hood into the Columbia, free and easy.

The first record we have about the Sandy was the journal of Captain Meriwether Lewis and Lieutenant William Clark in 1805 as their expedition rowed down the Columbia River toward the sea. They noticed that off in the distance to the south was Mount Hood. Immediately to their left was a river that appeared to have lost its way. The river was only inches deep as it flattened out into an immense sand bar at the river's mouth three miles long and half a mile wide.

"I attempted to wade this stream and to my astonishment found the bottom a quick sand, and impassable," wrote Clark in his journal on November 3, 1805. Not surprisingly, they named the river the Quicksand River. Later the name was altered to what it is today.

What the explorers did not know in 1805 was that the Sandy and Mount Hood were closely intertwined, and there had been an eruption on the mountain a decade earlier—but not a violent eruption like that of Mount St. Helens in 1980. Instead, at some point in the mid-1790s, molten lava oozed out of the dome of Mount Hood and in turn caused avalanche debris and pyroclastic flows with gas, ash, and melted snow and ice that gushed down through the river valley. This slurry of rock, mud, and water knocked over large stands of Douglas fir and red cedar, and today as you float down the river, you can see logs stuck in the high sand banks, remnants of this volcanic activity. It took more than a decade to flush all that sediment out to the Columbia, and that is why the expedition saw the broad expanse of sand bars, so unstable that they could not be walked upon. A few years later the river removed most of the excess sediment, much like the Toutle River, which flushed out the sediment after the Mount St. Helens eruption in 1980.

While the river may have expelled most of the tons of mud and sand from the early 1800s, the shores of the river are still thick with sand—

and quicksand. I know. I have been stuck in quicksand there a couple of times, and, believe me, it is not fun. One time on a drift-boat fishing trip downriver of Oxbow Park, we beached the boat and got out to fish from the bank. As I walked along the sandy beach, suddenly my left leg got sucked down into the soft sand. I pulled my leg out forcefully and in the process I wrenched my left leg painfully and could barely walk the remainder of the day. A few days later the back of my thigh was black and blue with internal bruising.

Another time I got stuck in quicksand up to my knees. I was fishing alone from the bank and had hiked down to the shore. One boot and then the other suddenly got stuck in the wet sand. I wiggled about in my waders trying to get at least one leg out, but it seemed that whenever I moved my feet I just got stuck deeper and deeper. I looked around and realized that no one else was around, the late afternoon was quickly darkening, and there were swirls of snow in the air. Earlier in the day drift boats occasionally floated by that stretch of water, but by late afternoon all those boats had already gone downriver toward the lower boat ramp at Dabney State Park. I was indeed alone even though I was only a few miles from a major metropolitan area. Down in the canyon there was no cellphone reception. The nights are long in the Pacific Northwest winter, and if I stayed stuck in the wet sand overnight, I would have been hypothermic and maybe dead by the time the first fishing boat drifted by in the morning. What a sorry sight that would have been for a couple of boat anglers to look out in the misty morning at the edge of the shore and see a tall guy standing bolt upright, rigid, frozen, like a statue, his wadered body stuck in the sand. The image was not a pleasant one, so I struggled ever so carefully, wiggling my feet back and forth and then up and down a little. Finally, I got one foot out of the muck and then the other one.

Aside from the quicksand, the Sandy River has been a good friend to me. I caught my first winter steelhead on the Sandy. I have had many fine floats down the Sandy in my drift boat with passengers from schoolteachers to insurance salesmen and even an ex-congressman. I have explored up and down the banks of the river from the Forest Service ranger station at Zig Zag all the way down to Tad's Chicken N' Dumplins restaurant near the mouth. My drinking water comes from a tributary of the Sandy called the Bull Run River. For many years the river provided electricity for my home. My son and I once climbed the summit of Mount Hood, at 11,250 feet, and looked down at the river's headwaters. At the mouth the Sandy still sputters its way out into the Columbia, weaving its way through shifting sand bars: And just off those bars, I and other salmon fishermen anchor their boats in the Columbia in the hope of catching a fall Chinook.

The Sandy is an urban river, but its rugged canyon just to the east of the Portland area makes it appear that it is not; in places it is more like a wilderness river. As close as it is to a metropolitan area of more than two million people, the fifty-six-mile undammed Sandy is a clean, cold river, the water crashing over rocks in some places and in other spots spreading out into smooth flat runs. The river's headwaters trickle out of the blue-hued Reid Glacier and Sandy Glacier on the flanks of Mount Hood. Unlike most rivers, you can see the river's source and its mouth in a single glance: The mouth of the Sandy has an elevation of fifty feet and is at the northeast edge of the Portland metropolitan area. Interstate 84 crosses the Sandy on a bridge at the mouth, and if you look up to the southeast, you can see Mount Hood, the river's source, nearly two miles high. The terrain slopes steeply, as you might expect, from glaciers and snowfields to patches of white-colored avalanche lilies in the alpine meadows. Farther down the slope sprout the white-tasseled bear grass, broad-leafed skunk cabbage, and dainty three-petal trillium flowers. In places there are wild, spindly rhododendrons, their pink blossoms peppered against a curtain of forest green: Douglas fir, Engelmann spruce, silver fir, and western hemlock. Along the river are the red cedars, their straight grain trees perfect for splitting shingles, the wood excellent from siding to fences because of its ability to ward off insects and thereby stave off rot in this wet, damp climate. Alders line the river from the upper reaches of the watershed to its confluence, brushy in the summer and in the winter a forest of skeletons, defrocked, silent, waiting for the buds to appear in the spring. Underfoot is a thicket of ferns, salal, salmonberry, and Oregon grape.

One damp March day, when the alders had not yet leafed out, I drove to Dodge Park, not far from the aptly named town of Sandy. I knew I was not going to be alone as there are only a few roads in that particular stretch of the river that snake down into the canyon and go all the way to the bottom of the river. At the park there is some access along the river, and usually there is company. I had only a few hours to fish that afternoon and I thought this might be a good spot, despite the competition. I was fishing for steelhead, and on the west side of the Cascades, steelhead enter freshwater as early as November. They migrate upriver to their spawning grounds and spawn usually in March or April. These fish are called winter-run steelhead. East of the Cascades, steelhead enter freshwater as early as June and spawn usually in March. These summer-run steelhead swim much farther upstream from the ocean than do the winter-run fish—as far as up the Wenatchee River in Washington, the Clearwater River in Idaho, and the Grande Ronde in Oregon—hundreds of miles from saltwater.

I used my jig setup with a casting rod, level-wind reel, bobber, and jig, even though I usually fish with flies. Fishing for winter steelhead on a fly is very challenging unless the conditions are just right. The flows in the winter are usually high, making it difficult to get the fly down, plus the fish do not want to move around much due to the cold water temperatures. You need to put your fly or lure right in front of the fish's nose, and the best way to do that is usually not with a fly but with a jig or a spoon. Also, summer steelhead linger for six months or more in freshwater before they spawn, so those fish are available to the anglers longer than are the winter fish that scoot up the river more quickly.

The act of fly fishing for winter steelhead is difficult, too, because most fly anglers utilize sink-tip lines to get the flies down near the bottom where the fish are. And for some reason the fish also seem to want large, and sometimes weighted, flies. To make matters more challenging, the winter fly angler has to cast out farther into the run due to the greater flows, and casting sink-tips with large flies is more difficult than in the summer when the angler is able to cast a smaller fly on a floating or intermediate tip. Plus, the really fast sink-tips used in the winter are like anchor rope, and there is no mending with such tips. All in all, I fish exclusively with flies for summer-run steelhead. In the winter, however, I use flies when the conditions are favorable, such as when the river levels are lower and the water temperatures are higher. But when that is not possible, I often use a jig or a spoon where the angler can put something right in front of the fish instantly. Actually, many steelhead fly anglers nowadays use jigs and strike indicators in both the summer and winter and they call it fly fishing—though it really is fly rod fishing and not fly fishing. But that is fine by me as I do not believe in splitting hairs about the definition of the term *fly fishing*. (Technically, a jig is not a fly because the lead is molded onto the hook. Tying barbell eyes on a hook, like a Clouser Minnow, is considered to be a fly. Wrapping twenty turns of lead on a #4 stonefly nymph hook is still considered to be a fly. But tying some wispy bit of marabou on a jig hook is not considered to be a fly. Things can get pretty anal in the fly-fishing department. Some stalwart tiers eschew using plastic bodies or foam. I have asked them if we should go up into the Mesabi Iron Range in Minnesota, dig the ore ourselves, and forge our own hooks.)

When I do pick up my fly rod, I prefer swinging the fly and not nymphing with heavily weighted flies or jigs. To me, an across and slightly downstream cast, a few mends, and a long swing is the epitome of steelhead fly fishing. When the fish strikes, you feel as though a freight train just clobbered your fly. But when those winter conditions make it difficult, or where there is little or no swing type of water available, then I think nothing of putting something else on the end of the line.

On that cold, damp day in March on the Sandy, I drove across the old steel bridge and pulled into the parking lot at the park. I put on my knee-high rubber boots, coat, hat, and gear and headed down to the water. At a low rise the rocky beach fell away down to the shore, and I studied the water. There were four anglers on the drift: It was a long one so there was room for all and the water color was excellent—steelhead green. I was sure that there were fish in the river, but the question was where exactly they were because the Sandy is a good-sized river. I walked along the rocky bank threading my way through some willow saplings and took my place near the lower end of the drift. The river's current speed was about the same as a fast walk. A "drift" on a section of a river is where the whitewater slows into a swirling but flat surface, probably about five feet deep or so. Most drifts deepen into a pool midway down and then the river shallows out into a tailout. In that particular drift the other anglers had positioned themselves in the upper and middle reaches of the 150-yard drift. I decided that I would cast a jig out into a mid-river slot at the lower end of the pool and then work my way down toward the tailout.

I glanced upstream and checked out my fishing companions. I noticed that their terminal gear was brightly colored: pink worms, roe, ghost shrimp, orange corkies, flame-red jigs. I suspected that they—and others—had fished through that drift all day long, and I was not optimistic because of the intense competition. But the river itself was in good shape: The river level was not too high or too low, and the color was just a bit off so it was not cloudy and not crystal clear either. And I really wanted a fish. To be precise, I did not just want to go fishing—I wanted to catch a fish as I had had a run of bad luck lately when it came to winter steelhead.

With everyone else using brightly colored tackle, I decided to do something different. I selected one of my own jigs that I had tied up a few weeks earlier using a black marabou feather and a kingfisher blue-colored hackle. A jig is a single hook with a round small lead ball near the eye of the hook. The shank of the hook is attached to any number of materials—usually some type of feather. Marabou feathers, in particular, are popular for fly tiers and jig tiers because when immersed in the water marabou feathers ungulate and animate the fly or the jig. Originally, these feathers were taken from the marabou stork, but now these feathers, called semi plumes, are plucked from turkeys and are dyed a variety of colors. These long, thin flexible semi plumes do not interlock the barbs of the feathers as do flight feathers and thereby are as wispy as they can be.

I tied on the dark jig and pinched a split-shot on the line. I cast the rig out and after a few times I felt that the placement was good. I tried to keep the white foam bobber level as it drifted by, hopefully, dangling the jig below a foot or two off the bottom. I cast out and then immediately mended the line, much like in fly fishing, so the line would not drag the jig along. The toughest thing about jig-fishing for steelhead is keeping the bobber perpendicular to the surface of the water so the jig moves drag-free, just along with the speed of the current. It is difficult, at least to me, but this sight-fishing is always exciting, the bobber floating with the current, ever ready to be yanked under the water with a big tug. I had my heavier steelhead rod along and twelve-pound leader because some

Chinook salmon were starting to enter the river, too, and I did not want to be under-gunned in case a salmon took my jig instead of a steelhead. A spring Chinook salmon weighs twice as much as a steelhead.

I slowly moved down the riverbank trying to "vacuum" that stretch of water. I cast in close, then out in the middle, and then toward the far side. The jig ran through those imaginary lanes over and over, so if a silvery fish was in that area, it would at least notice my offering. As I went downstream foot by foot, I glanced around at my fellow anglers. They were all fishing with the same method using a bobber setup, but I did not see any action— just the same cast, mend, float, and retrieve.

For the next hour I continued to cast out the jig again—and again. I moved slowly down the bank putting the jig in a slightly different spot each time. After each cast I mended the line a couple of times to keep the line from dragging the jig. I carefully watched the bobber as it floated by with the current. One time the bobber got sucked down into a swirl, disappearing from view, and then it popped out again. Every now and again the bobber got stuck in a back eddy, and once or twice I had to raise the rod and pull the bobber back into the current. Near the end of the float where the bottom shallowed out, I felt the rod shudder.

"What's that darned rock doing at the end of my line?" I said to myself.

The star drag was set pretty tight, but all the same I noticed that the line was slowly running off the spool. Then the rod tip throbbed up and down hard.

"Hot damn!" I shouted. "It's not a rock!"

It was a fish and it thrashed about on the surface. It was a good, strong fish. There were no aerial acrobatics as steelhead sometimes do. It was a Mexican standoff type of fish: It did not take a lot of line or jump, but it did not budge either. Eventually, I pumped the rod upwards, and then when I eased the rod down, I reeled in a little line. I had a broad grin on my face: The silent but tactile communication between fish and man had once again been re-established after weeks of going without a strike. Now it was all about the fight: The predatory instinct kicked in and there was no thinking about anything else other than fighting the fish. Pinpoint concentration.

I imagined that the fish was trying to keep its head down near the bottom. I, on the other hand, kept the rod tip up, hoping that the fish would raise its head so I could better control it. I also imagined that the fish did not know that we were connected. All it knew was that something or somebody was trying to drag it out of the depths toward the shallows.

By then I had attracted a crowd on the bank. After all it was a county park and there were both anglers and non-anglers around. At such times I always get nervous and try not to be a fool, because with a strong fish on the line most anything can happen. Normally, fishing is not a spectator sport, but then and there it was—and I was the performer.

"It's awfully stubborn, maybe it's a Chinook," I said to one of the other anglers who came over to help me out.

Slowly, I got the fish in closer and closer. I backed away from the water bringing the fish still closer. Finally, my new angling friend and I both saw a silver flash, a wink in the cold, green-tinged current. It was a steelhead, lithe and slender, not deep-bellied like a salmon. At the same time the fish saw us and bolted. The line sizzled off the spool and the fish hunkered down in the deep water.

Again, I pumped the rod upward, and as I lowered it, I reeled in some more line. Slowly, I regained the line back inch by inch. Anglers, mothers, and kids were all standing around looking at me, the bowed rod, and the fish. Finally, the fish came in close to the bank.

"What a beautiful fish!" said someone in the crowd. I certainly agreed: It was a mint-bright steelhead holding in the cold water. My helper coaxed it toward the rocky beach and I held the rod high.

"There's the fin; it's wild," said my helper. According to the angling regulations, we had to release the fish because it had an intact adipose fin and it was wild, not a hatchery-reared fish, and that was fine with me. If the adipose fin had been clipped, it would have meant that it was a hatchery fish and we could legally kill it and enjoy a delicious steelhead dinner. The fish had put on quite a display. I surmised that it weighed in at about eight pounds and bright as a button. In a few weeks it would veer off into a tributary creek, its flanks turning pink to red and violet, and before long it would find a mate and spawn, the translucent orange eggs sinking down into the female's graveled nest. A few weeks later the tiny alevin would emerge, and they would rear in the Sandy's clean, cold water, then migrate to the ocean as a smolt and begin the cycle all over again. Unlike salmon, not all steelhead die after spawning, and those not too exhausted from their efforts sometimes go back downriver all the way to the ocean to once again feed on the shrimp and squid and little baitfish. Once I caught one of these returning Sandy River steelhead, called a kelt, and it was a sorry-looking fish: There was no zip to it whatsoever. I was sorry I hooked it—a dark, emaciated ghost of what it was a few months earlier. I released it and never knew whether or not it ever made it back to the ocean.

After we got the hook out of the fish's jaw, my helper cradled the fish's head and I held the wrist of its tail while it rested in the shallow water. It was tired but not defeated, because the word *defeat* is a human characteristic irrelevant to a fish. The fish was simply tired; it would revive quickly in the cold water. Sometimes when the shallow water has little current to it, the angler can hold the fish and stimulate the fish's "breathing" movement by moving it back and forth, allowing the gills to pump oxygenated water into its respiratory system. With my grip gently around the fish's body, I noticed that its flesh was firm and muscular. Then I looked into its unblinking eyes and there was nothing there: flat, vacuous, and dark. Eyes are the window of the soul, and while this may be true with people, it did not appear to be so with fish. While a steelhead is a superb game fish, a fish is only a fish, an instinctive animal seeing only its immediate surroundings, unable to animate that which is from within.

I gave my phone camera to one of the others on the bank and one of the mothers snapped the picture of me and the fish. In less than a minute, the fish wiggled once, then twice, and then scooted away, swimming off into the deeper water.

"Nice fish," said several people in the crowd.

"Thanks," I said.

The crowd dispersed and I examined my rig. The line held and so did the Duncan's loop knot, but the bend in the hook had nearly straightened out. I was damned lucky I landed that fish! Well, I know now what brand of hooks not to buy.

Lightning never strikes twice, but just in case I clipped off the damaged jig and tied on another dark-colored one and cast it out into the current. I cast again, then again. Where there is one fish, there is usually another one or two nearby. Yet at the same time, I did not feel the urgency of hooking a fish as I did earlier. Then I really wanted to connect with something other than slack line. I wanted a physical communication between myself and a wild creature, not just a photograph of a salmon jumping the falls or the screech of an owl or a quick glance at a black-tailed deer walking through the woods. I wanted more: a taut line knifing through the water, a throbbing rod, its cork handle pushing into my belly, the backing burning off the spool. But there was not the same urgency now compared to an hour ago. With that fine fish on the bank, I was somewhat satiated, not drained at all, but ... well ... satisfied, a smile on my face, the furrows on my brow a little less pronounced, the tension of the pre-strike casting gone.

The drizzle continued, dribbling off my hat brim: falling raindrops, falling everywhere, on the foliage, on the rocky bank, on the surface of the river—and on me. On these northwestern days I feel sodden with the humidity surrounding me, soaking into my core despite my slicker, wool shirt, wool trousers, and wool socks. A Montana friend of mine who was visiting once said that 20 degrees in Bozeman feels warmer than 40 degrees in Portland. Sometimes I am so intent on the fishing that I fail to realize that I am cold. The best indication of the cold is when I try to tie on a new jig or take my water bottle out of my pack. Then I fumble. My fingers barely move: They are thick, stupid fingers that barely can grasp the simplest thing.

Suddenly, a rainbow appeared right over the river some three hundred yards downriver from me. The rainbow—colored violet at the bottom and red at the top—glowed in the dying mist of an Oregon March day, the sky capped with gray clouds, the banks studded with naked alders and vine maple. In May a colorful and cheerful spring day can sometimes wake the dead, but in early March?

March is always a dreary month in the Northwest with winter fading and spring just a promise. Now this lackluster month blazed a neon arch over the waters. The rainbow marched upriver toward me.

Dumbfounded, I stepped back. It kept marching toward me. Maybe the pot of gold is on my way! I froze and didn't move. I blinked my eyes and stared again.

What a sight!

And so close to me!

I felt as though I could reach out and touch it. I am always flummoxed whenever I see a rainbow bright and in close. There are many faces of water from rivers to raindrops to glaciers—all composed of the substance called water. However, unlike the other faces of water, a rainbow has no substance. It is there but it is not there. Even invisible water vapor has substance: You can feel it on a muggy day. You cannot touch it or see it, but it is there, waiting for the right conditions to condense and turn into visible water droplets. A rainbow, however, has no substance: It is an image, not an object. It is the optical effect of the sun's light shining upon millions of raindrop mirrors. It is of interest to us solely because of its beauty and mystery. It is no wonder that our ancestors thought that rainbows were supernatural creations. Ancient Babylonians thought the rainbow was the fiancé of the rain. In South America some native tribes believed that the rainbow was husband to the moon. Some cultures believed rainbows to be a sign of good luck; others believed them to be a sign of bad luck.

Suddenly, *my* rainbow collapsed. Its bright shards dissolved into the mist. The air between the canyon walls was once again clear, without color, and I missed the display of color and wished it would reappear, but of course it did not.

I reeled in the line and put the jig in the keeper. I grabbed my small tackle box filled with winter steelhead gear including colorful jigs, floats, split-shot, pliers, knife, nippers, snap swivels, barrel swivels, homemade spinners threaded with ruby-colored glass beads on slender steel shafts, and nickel hammered spoons. I walked up to the bank and sat down on a smooth, flat rock and thought about the wistful rainbow and my bright steelhead. The two were not dissimilar: They were both rainbows, each in their own way. Steelhead are simply an ocean-going rainbow trout; along its flanks are the colors of the rainbow, the lateral line pink or rose or blush or sometimes scarlet, fading onto a field of silver or steely blue, or emerald green or olive.

A steelhead and a resident rainbow trout are genetically the same, according to the experts. When they are juveniles they are virtually indistinguishable. But when those rainbow trout go out to sea, something happens. Maybe it is the saltwater. As they grow larger and larger, feeding on squid and shrimp in the North Pacific, their coloration changes into a mint-bright silver color and they become more streamlined. A twenty-six-inch resident rainbow trout in freshwater is usually fatter than a twenty-six-inch steelhead. When steelhead return to their spawning waters and come into freshwater, they change color again. My Sandy River fish had not changed much, for it was a winter fish and it had traveled quickly from saltwater to Dodge Park. Its topside was dark but the sides were chrome.

Some summer steelhead remain in freshwater for as long as six months or more and their silvery bodies change—like a rainbow emerging out of the mist. Depending on how long they have been in freshwater, their backs and upper sides begin to darken into many colors from olive to brown to dark blue. They have little dark spots on their sides. And along their lateral line is the rainbow, the hallmark of a rainbow trout. Sometimes the rainbow stripe along the flank glows with a rosy pink, fading into a silvery blue background. Other fish, especially the males, have a brilliant red stripe on a dark-spotted field of dark green or brown. And the bright stripe runs all the way up into the gill plates, the color uniting the head and body. The fish not only change color week by week on their way upriver, but their coloration changes by the minute after they are landed and killed. Within a short time of when a fish is clubbed, the iridescence starts to fade, the once-radiant shower of colors dim, the sheen on the fish's slippery surface changes from gloss to matte. Like a rainbow in the sky, the steelhead's rainbow is also transitory: silver in the salt, pink along its flanks in freshwater, and dark and lusterless on the spawning grounds.

I stood up, adjusted my hat, and looked out at the river. It was later in the afternoon, almost early evening, and the muted sun was dimmer by the minute. It was a typical Northwest winter day, cold and damp, but I was not uncomfortable. There was a warm glow of satisfaction inside me, like the warmth of a campfire, maple coals flickering, radiant in an iron fire ring at camp. With a wonderful premium game fish at my feet just a short time ago, I decided that it was as good as it gets. It was time to go home and fish another day.

Chapter Five

Hellroaring Headwater

Not far from the Sandy River is another Columbia River tributary, one that lies on the Washington side of the Columbia. That river flows off the glaciers of yet another volcanic Cascade mountain, the second-highest peak in the state of Washington. Named after the second president of the United States, Mount Adams dominates the state's southern Cascades with its bulk—and its beauty—and much of its eastern slopes drain into a little-known river called the Klickitat.

The Klickitat and the Sandy share many similarities: Both rivers are short, less than one hundred miles long each. Both are undammed and their waters are clean and cold. Both have robust salmon and steelhead runs. Both flow into the Columbia. Both are closely intertwined with volcanic mountains: Mount Hood and Mount Adams. Both mountains were formed about half a million years ago. Both have been heavily glaciated, the ice smoothing out the jagged lava flows that had oozed out of the restless mountains over thousands of years.

Though similar in some ways, the two rivers and two mountains are as dissimilar as can be. Both the Sandy River and Mount Hood are heavily populated by fishermen, skiers, campers, mountain climbers, and vacationers. People can drive on a paved highway all the way up to the alpine meadows at Timberline Lodge, one of the most splendid mountain lodges in the West. From the steps of the lodge, more than ten thousand climbers attempt to scale the summit of Mount Hood every year. For its part the Sandy is filled with anglers for much of the year searching for salmon and steelhead. In the summer when the fishing slows down, the river is filled with rafters and swimmers. On hot summer days thousands of youngsters, and some not so young, cool off in the Sandy's refreshing waters.

In contrast, there are no roads close to the alpine meadows of Mount Adams, and there are no lodges nearby either. To reach the timberline you have to hike. The two mountains look different, too: the one pointed and angular; the other heavily shouldered, massive, much like Mount Rainier. While campers and hikers enjoy themselves in the Mount Adams area during summer weekends, the area is not as populated compared to Mount Hood. Likewise, the Klickitat has its share of fishermen seeking steelhead and salmon, too, but not near as many as on the Sandy because the Sandy is much closer to Portland than is the Klickitat. To the north the Klickitat is a long way from the populous Seattle-Tacoma area. In many sections of the Klickitat, an angler can find solitude. The upper section of the river is even more remote, and much of the area is off-limits to all but the members of the Yakama Nation, an Indian reservation larger than the state of Rhode Island. Also, most of the east side of Mount Adams is owned by the tribe; however, some of that area is open to non-Indians for camping, hiking, and fishing.

While it is difficult to actually venture into the upper reaches of the Klickitat as a non–tribal member, nonetheless you can peek over the edge of the river's headwaters as you hike along the Pacific Crest Trail between Mount Adams and Mount Rainier. East of the divide, the snowmelt, rain, and springs trickle down the slope from rills to rivulets to creeks to the Klickitat. And at the very upper end of the river's headwaters at Cispus Pass lies the Goat Rocks, a jagged horizon of dark-colored basalt, patches of snowy cirques, green meadows, and icy-blue tarns. At the summit of Gilbert Peak at 8,184 feet, the rocky ridges are bare and the more gentle slopes are covered with snow. To the east and south of the bowl-shaped pass, the snowfields begin to melt in the late spring every year and trickle into the nascent Klickitat. A few miles downstream Huckleberry Creek and Elkhorn Creek flow into the Klickitat from the west and its icy waters flatten out into McCormick Meadows.

Farther to the south other Klickitat headwaters flow down the eastern flanks of Mount Adams, and one day my wife and I went there to check it out. We drove north of Trout Lake and paid a small fee to enter the tribal lands at the southeast corner of the mountain. We camped at a small lake for two nights, and one day we took a day hike to Bird Creek meadows, a lovely spot, the kind of place where you would expect Heidi to skip by herding along a few goats, yodeling to her heart's content. The meadow was thick with wildflowers from magenta-colored Indian paintbrush to purple shooting stars, red columbine, and yellow glacier lilies. The heather and huckleberry bushes were thick; and poking up in little clumps here and there were ancient-looking alpine firs, windswept, like little old men in overcoats bent over and shivering with the wind at their backsides.

Over the lip of the bucolic meadows was a raw, recently glaciated watercourse aptly named Hellroaring Creek. At first glance it appeared to be a mining operation, but it was not. Instead, it was nature's open wound, a ravine of rock, dirt, and gravel, the tan-colored muddy waters of the Hellroaring racing downward. Way up on the slope of the creek, above a little waterfall, was a patch of grass dotted with grazing mountain goats, just white specks on a patch of green brushed across the barren mountain clad with rock, snow, and ice. There at the base of the flanks of the mountain was the Mazama Glacier, which in the summer melts and its milky glacial waters flow down its moraine into the Hellroaring, which, in turn, flows into the Klickitat. Just to the north over the next ridge, called the Ridge of Wonders, was Big Muddy Creek, which flows out of the Klickitat Glacier, the melt funneling down the mountain to the Klickitat. And over the next ridge, called Battlement Ridge, was yet another watercourse carved out of yet another glacier named Rusk Glacier. Its melt flows into the self-same creek, which, in turn, flows through the Avalanche Valley and later into the Klickitat, too. I would have liked to have hiked over the Ridge of Wonders and beyond, but there were few trails and in that glacial country going off-trail can be arduous and downright dangerous, so I had to be satisfied with seeing only one of the Klickitat's glacial headwaters up close—the Hellroaring.

And that was fine by me. I have seen the Klickitat's headwater from various vantage points, and, to me, finding the sources of rivers is always satisfying. The upper reaches of the Klickitat are much like other mountain streams and resemble a staircase. These steps are really miniature dams and are built out of fallen trees and blocked boulders. The reason there are so many fallen trees and blocked boulders in headwaters country are twofold: First, most headwater areas are forested, and due to wind, erosion, fire, disease, and just plain old age, a lot of trees fall down. Second, headwater areas are usually steep, and so the resulting streams are swift. The current in these streams washes gravel and sand from around the edges of the boulders. Without the support of the surrounding gravel and sand, the boulders roll into the channel and block the stream, causing a step or dam. The water plunges down, step by step, and scours out the streambed below creating a pool. Later as the gradient flattens, the pools become deeper and longer. The current slows and deposits some of its suspended load, like sugar crystals suspended in a cup of tea. It is this entrained gravel and sand and clay that sculpt the rocks. Call it liquid sandpaper. As the current slows, some of this suspended sediment falls to the river's floor. This lightens its water-borne load, speeds up, and creates a riffle. Gradually and seamlessly, a step and pool headwater stream morphs into a river of riffles and pools.

About seventy-five miles long, the Klickitat is a hurry-up river from its headwaters in the alpine country to the confluence of the Columbia where the elevation is eighty feet above sea level. It has no time for meanders or oxbows or long languid pools. It wants to get there quickly and that is what it does. There are two towns along the river: Lyle at the mouth and Klickitat some thirteen miles upriver. The upriver town once supported a number of lumber mills in the early 1900s, but the last mill was closed in 1994. A decade later the nearby Goldendale Aluminum plant on the Columbia was closed, too. While an economically troubled area nowadays, the river itself is healthy. After a heavy rainfall the river muddies-up some due to erosion. In the summer when the weather turns hot, the glaciers of the mountain begin to melt and flow down into Hell-roaring Creek and Big Muddy Creek and Rusk Creek, and that milky, suspended load of glacial till clouds the river. At such times fishermen, such as me, go somewhere else to fish. It is not because the fish are not there. They are still there, but it is difficult for the fish to see the fly or lure when river visibility is less than a few inches.

Anglers are fussy about visibility, or "viz," as some say. With two inches of "viz," you might as well go somewhere else to fish. With a foot or more of visibility, the fishing could be okay. However, when you can see through six feet of water and see every stone at the bottom, then there is too much "viz." Transparency may be a fine attribute in politics and finance, but it is not good for the fish. If you can see the fish, then the fish can see you. And to a fish a human being means trouble. Fish seek cover and protection from predators such as people, herons, larger fish, mergansers, and otters. Fish like shaded waters. They like to hide under cutbanks, under rock shelves, and under the riparian tree canopy. Fish are most active in low light, such as at dawn and dusk and on overcast days. Fish have no eyelids and no sunglasses, so when the river is clear and the sky is clear and the sun is bright, they hunker deep near the bottom, wary and unresponsive to even a well-tied fly.

One early October day I went fishing on the Klickitat not far from the town of Klickitat. There the river is no longer a headwater river, but then again it is not a meandering river either. It has a good clip to it with whitewater riffles interspersed with long, soft-water runs where the current moves along at the pace of a man's walking speed. On that day the fall Chinook salmon were in thick, thrashing about, and one almost knocked me down as I was wading thigh-deep trying to cast out toward the far bank. Few of the spawning salmon appeared to be bright and worthy of eating, so I did not try to catch them. Once their flanks were silver and their flesh firm, but now, far from saltwater, they were colored with tan, yellow, and pink blotches, their backs darkened, some with white fungus on the tips of the dorsal fin and the tail. In some places over in the shallows, they were already on the redds. And a few had already drifted off the spawning beds, floating into the back eddies, lifeless and table fare only for eagles, gulls, and raccoons.

The spawning salmon were simply a nuisance for me that day, because Chinook salmon are double the size of steelhead. Both salmon and steelhead often like to hold in tailouts where the current is not as swift as in the upper reaches of a run. When the salmon are running, they push the steelhead out of those areas into swifter waters. That means the steelhead angler needs to adapt and fish the faster water.

Despite the numerous salmon, the month of October is a wonderful time of year to go steelhead fishing because the steelhead are almost always there. On the first day of October, I may be wearing a T-shirt and a broad-brimmed hat for the sun. By the last day of the month, I might put on a warm coat and wool stocking cap to ward off the cold. In October the leaves are as transient as are the temperatures: At the beginning of the month, the leaves are bonded to the branches, but by the end of the month, most of the leaves are long gone, the foliage stripped from the branches, a crazy-quilt of dark, naked limbs like an unruly Jackson Pollock painting.

On the middle and lower sections of the Klickitat, the scrub oak trees are interspersed with ponderosa pines. Leaves and needles covered the duff as I hiked across the ground toward the river. The oak acorns litter the floor, a staple for squirrels, deer, and wild turkeys. The river is hemmed in by basalt cliffs much of the way, and so the valley has little arable land save for a few acres of pasture. The country is a narrow transition band between the Cascade Mountains and the sagebrush treeless country to the east. Some would say that the canyon itself has little value, except for the timber in its upper reaches. Above the canyon is the Goldendale plateau where crops spout out of a fertile soil, a soil that is richer than down in the rocky canyon, a soil that has a kind of amiability to it. Most of us are more comfortable with arable land: tidy farms with pastures, wheatfields, row crops, cattle, orchards, tractors, silos, fences, barns, houses, and outbuildings. It is a restful horizontal land.

When the land, such as the Klickitat canyon, suddenly goes vertical, the Earth's skin begins to wrinkle. At the edge of the plateau, down into the bottom of the canyon, there is a deep, ragged gash. While of little use to others, to me the river and its canyon produces something beyond economics, and that is why I was there on that day in October, wading knee deep in the river, my studded felt boot soles scratching the river cobble, down at rock bottom, down where erosion and other forces had cleaved their ways deep into the Earth's gnarly crust.

On that October day the fallen leaves snagged my fly maddeningly time after time. I stripped in line, picked up the impaled leaves, and threw them out on the water where they drifted downstream and dropped to the bottom. Where the current slowed near the bank, the leaves piled one upon another at the muddy bottom, a mat of orange, tan, and yellow soggy detritus. Once the leaves enlivened the land and shaded it so mercifully, but now, their task completed, their pliant green leaves were tough and brittle, their chlorophyll extinguished for the year.

Call it the Moon of Falling Leaves—October is a special month to many of us. In January or July the world is much the same week in and week out. It is cold at the beginning of January and it is still cold at the end of the month; likewise, it is warm in July all month long. But in October the natural world lives and dies in a few weeks. October is a month of transcendence. You want to hold onto every sharp, sunny October day, wringing the juice out of it while the calendar moves relentlessly by.

On a tributary of Idaho's Big Wood River is a monument to Ernest Hemingway. The inscription is from a 1939 eulogy Hemingway wrote for a friend killed in a hunting mishap.

> Best of all he loved the fall,
> The leaves yellow on the cottonwoods,
> Leaves floating on the trout streams,
> And above the hills
> The high blue windless skies ...
> Now he will be part of them forever.

Thirty-one days are not enough for October.

On that fine October day on the Klickitat River near the town of Klickitat in the County of Klickitat, I thought about what type of fly I should tie on to the tippet. I had fished through several runs without success and it was now late in the afternoon, the sun behind the tall ridge, the water's surface like rippling glass. I had tied on a dark concoction of my own called Midnight Fire, with four little white rubber legs tied to the shank. In the past fish have taken this fly, but not today. I also tied on my standard bright repertoire fly, Brad's Brat, an orange body ribbed with silver tinsel. I found no luck with that one either. I sat down at the edge of the shore, the long grasses sprouting through the mud, the bushes hard up against me. I took a swig from my small water bottle. I was tired with the wading and casting, although the weather was splendid, warm earlier in the day and now cool with the fading daylight.

I thought about how other anglers had been telling me that in the fall the summer steelhead often revert to their days as little trout when they once chased insects in the rivers of their youth. After a while those juvenile fish migrate downriver to the ocean, stay there for several years, and then return to their natal waters. After being inland for a few months, a steelhead's saltwater memory grows dim. Long gone are the days of chasing shrimp and squid out on the broad Pacific Ocean. Now as they rest in the cold waters of the Klickitat, the fish look for inland prey: nymphs, flies, sculpins, even ants.

Serendipity.

Some five feet from the bank, I saw a large, amber-colored fly, fluttering to beat the band. As a trout angler, I recognized it as an October Caddis, one of the largest caddisflies in the West. Compared to most other caddisflies, the October Caddis at an inch long is a hearty meal for a trout—or even a steelhead. As a trout angler, I have not had much success with the adult October Caddis version, but the fish seemed to like eating the pupae version.

The October Caddis is an interesting bug. Its larvae excrete a type of silk from their salivary glands that bind together pebbles and grains of sand to build their tiny houses. They attach themselves to stones at the bottom of rivers and streams. They peek out of their homes and feed on diatoms and algae. Eventually, they close the doors of their houses and pupate by spinning more silk to wrap themselves up into a cocoon. Using a pair of mandibles, they eventually cut open their rock houses, also called periwinkles, and swim up to the surface where they cast off their skin and emerge as an air-breathing flying insect.

While wondrous as this journey may be, to the fly fisherman, the point of it is where and when do the fish feed on those tasty bugs? Generally, the fish find that the most readily available time to catch bugs is when the pupae swim up from the bottom of the river to the surface. While they are agile swimmers, it takes time to get up to the top, shed their skin, and spread their wings. And that is when the fish are best able to ambush the bugs.

After seeing several October Caddis flying along the shore, I nosed into my fly box and found a pupal pattern: a little longer than half an inch with a burnt-orange body and a dark brown thorax. The fly was also weighted so it would sink.

The light was fading and I had less than an hour to fish, so I began casting out the pupa in the middle section of the run. I cast it out upstream, let it dead drift down through the current, and then I let it swing across the flow toward shore. The water was deep close in next to the bushes, and I was able to wade out only four feet or so from the bank. As I waded, I had to navigate the basketball-sized rocks that studded the river's bottom. The water had a slight tea-colored tint to it, and I could not peer very far into it so I had to use my feet as eyes and blindly bump from rock to rock. I had my wading staff along, tethered by a cord to my waist, and I poked at river's bottom using my third leg. Some people think fly fishing is a graceful endeavor—and it can be at times—but much of the time it is downright awkward as you wade hip deep in the current desperately trying not to fall down.

It was late in the day and there was no one around. Before me was the river and the bushy shoreline. Overhead, I noticed a plane about ready to fly through some cumulus clouds, the jet engines ready to tear through the cumuli like paper. To the west, the horizon was starting to color with the approaching dusk. And back down into the cleft of the Earth's crust was the river itself, a million threads flowing along, its intricate hydrology barely noticed by me but known intimately to the fish, their sensory wherewithal as acute in the water as are the long antennas on the head of an October Caddis.

"There!" I said to myself. I saw a swirl on the surface of the water some twenty feet downstream. Then I felt the throbbing of the long, slender rod.

"Tight lines!" as they say in the business.

I backed up toward the bank so I could better manage the fish. It was hesitant at first, heavy bodied but not running off any line—yet. I could not see it and wondered if it was a steelhead or a Chinook. I had seen several salmon roll and break the surface in the same run. I imagined that some steelhead were probably also in the run as well, but I did not know. I was hoping it was a steelhead and not a worn-out salmon I would have had to tussle with . The weighty pull on the end of the line was gratifying as I had not had a fish on all day. Now the line hummed, tight as could be, and I hoped all my knots were up to snuff: nail knot, blood knots, Duncan's loop knot.

Finally, the fish seemed to realize that it was hooked into something strong. At that point I pumped the rod and tried to reel in some line, and the fish made a bee-line out into the main current, the line spooling off the reel, the gears singing in the way that a fisherman wants to hear.

"It must be a steelhead," I said to myself.

Gradually, I regained much of the line, and suddenly, I saw the fish in the dimly lit water: a torpedo-shaped fish some two-feet-plus long. Its back was dark, almost brown, a pink-blushed stripe on its flanks and the belly a pale-colored silver, almost white. The fish apparently saw me about the same time I saw it and it bolted, seeking deeper water, away from the large apparition that was hovering over the shallows.

As I got closer to the fish, I also was curious whether or not it was a wild or hatchery fish. Sometimes when a fish darts back and forth in the water, it is difficult to determine whether the fish is wild or not. As the fish tired, I got a better look at it and recognized that it was a "high fin," meaning that the adipose fin was intact. When I realized that the fish was a wild fish, I dropped my guard as I did not care whether or not the hook got loose. Had it been a hatchery fish, I would have done my best to make sure it got up on the bank, killed it, dressed it out, and later put it in the cooler of the car.

It took me longer than anticipated to beach the fish because there was no beach nearby. I had to bend down over the overhanging bushes next to shore and wade downstream some thirty feet where the vegetation opened. When I finally got there, thankfully there was a small rocky beach where I could slide the now-tired fish into the shallows. It was a buck steelhead, its angular head and its body a bit darker than I expected. I looked at the leader and saw the October Caddis fly stuck in the fish's lower jaw. The fly seemed large in my fly box, but in the steelhead's jaw it looked tiny. I examined the fly closely: The hook was not bent and the knot held.

I took out my pliers and easily pulled the fly out of the fish's jaw. While free of the hook and line, it still was tired, very tired, and so I held it in the shallow water and let it rest. It had been taken out of its element, resisted my efforts manfully, and needed to recoup from the fish-versus-man battle. It had moved relentlessly about for the past few years, from the tributary creeks of the Klickitat to far out into the cold North Pacific. It hunted prey from sardines to squid and, in turn, was prey to other creatures such as sea lions and killer whales. Fish biologists tell me that unlike many salmon that hug the coast, young steelhead leave their freshwater rivers behind and head straight out into the Pacific. Some researchers have found Idaho-reared steelhead in the nets of commercial fishermen far out on the broad North Pacific. Generally, there is less information about steelhead because most of the research has been spent on salmon and not steelhead. Salmon after all are considered a food fish. Steelhead, on the other hand, are a game fish because of their fighting abilities, fish that sometimes jump time and time again and delight anglers everywhere.

When reviving such a fish, some anglers are so enamored with their fish that they stroke it like a pet or give it a kiss. But I did not want to do anything like that. It would be demeaning to such a fine animal. I just gently held the fish so it could rest.

Suddenly, the fish flexed its muscular self and swam off into the depths. I got up off my knees, put my pliers away, walked over to a stump, and sat down. I felt satisfied. I examined the fly again and shook my head: little fly, big fish. I looked over to the west, along the horizon line of the canyon: The light had weakened and dusk had, indeed, arrived. October may feel like July in the middle of the day, but by early evening it regains its composure and becomes what it is. Another October Caddis fluttered by, looking perhaps ready to unload a mass of eggs down upon the moving water. The eggs would slowly drift their way down and lodge into the cracks and crevasses of the gravel and rocks. When the time was ripe, the newly born larvae would snuggle down onto the floor and unthinkingly begin to weave their pebble houses around themselves, anchoring down on the rocks, the water coursing through those little shelters.

In another month or two, the edges of the river would be glazed with ice. Farther upriver the first snows would have stuck to the duff and dirt and fir branches. Higher still, the newly fallen snow would have stuck to the surface of the ancient glaciers, frozen water upon frozen water. From Hellroaring Creek to the confluence of the Klickitat, the icy water would trickle out of the very mountainside. On either side of the creek would be a whitewashed landscape, rounded and softened as only a snowfall can accomplish.

And in another few months a small tributary of the Klickitat would host a steelhead buck resting in a pool, a tiny scar on its lower lip from the impact of a hook that I had dressed with some burnt-orange dubbing at my fly-tying bench in the basement of my home maybe years ago. The fish would be dark by then, thinner too, not the robust fish that once had tangled with a large predator and that once had felt a landlubber's touch. When ready, the buck would find a hen swollen with ripened eggs. She would build a nest and disgorge her eggs. He would slide over next to her, let loose his milt, and the fertilized eggs would sink down into the gravel.

If possible, he would try to return to the ocean, but likely he would not succeed. It is a long way from the slopes of Mount Adams to the Pacific Ocean, but you never know—he might make it.

CHAPTER SIX

The Falls

OREGON CITY IS THE TERMINUS OF THE OREGON TRAIL, THE TWO-thousand-mile route where tens of thousands of emigrants traveled westward from the 1840s to the early 1860s. Once Oregon's territorial capital until it was moved to Salem in 1851, Oregon City is on the banks of the Willamette River. There the pioneers parked their wagons, walked into the Office of Surveyor General for Oregon, and put in their homestead claims in the fertile Willamette Valley. The river itself is a bit less than two hundred miles in length and empties into the Columbia just northwest of Portland. Its many tributaries flow down from the west side of the Cascade Mountains into the valley. To the west of the valley, more tributaries flow down from the Coast Range and empty into the Willamette at various points there.

Salmon and steelhead have spawned and reared in the Willamette watershed for many centuries, although at some places waterfalls have prevented salmon from continuing up into their natal waters. However, in high water the vertical drop between the surface of the river and the top of the waterfall decreases, and in some cases the fish then are able to jump over the falls. Every spring the snowmelt in the mountains and the valley's abundant rainfall create an especially thundering volume of water down the Willamette at Oregon City where the river suddenly drops forty feet, creating the second-largest waterfall, by volume, in the nation. With those high water levels in the spring, historically salmon were able to get over the top of the waterfall and colonize the fish in the Willamette basin. Nowadays a fish ladder enables the fish to get over the falls easier.

Today the salmon school up at the base of the falls waiting for just the right water temperature and flow to ascend upwards into their spawning waters. And where salmon congregate so do the fishermen, from the days of the Indians who used long-handled hoop nets to hundreds of Portland-area anglers today with all manner of tackle, gear, and boats. The fishery is not a bucolic one: It is an urban fishery if ever there was one, and it has been that way for more than one hundred years. The closer to the falls, the greater are the crowds, with some boats pressing gunwale to gunwale almost all the way across the river—much like a pontoon bridge. Other boaters troll both upriver and downriver and still other anglers, called plunkers, fish from the bank.

While I have lived in the area for more than forty years, it was not until recently that I joined the fray, for generally when I go fishing, I like solitude. But after watching those anglers in their boats out on the Willamette trying to catch spring Chinook year after year, I finally succumbed—in part because I love to eat salmon and also in part because the Willamette fishery is close to home: It is where I live, where I feel rooted. (By the way, many gourmets claim that the best-tasting salmon in the world are the spring Chinook that migrate up the Columbia and into its tributaries, such as the Willamette.) To me, the best fishing experiences are those with some context, where there is a sense of place, something beyond just catching a fish. Some well-heeled anglers parachute into most anywhere in the world with rod and reel at the ready, bivouac at the lodge, catch some fish, and then jet out. Sometimes that can be fun, but then again when you know a landscape, its history, waters, fish, towns, and its people, the experience deepens beyond simply hooking a fish.

The Willamette Falls has been subjected to many alterations over the decades, including concrete revetments and massive, unsightly industrial buildings alongside the banks. Nonetheless, those falls are absolutely stunning: the green-white water pouring over the horseshoe-shaped rock ledges some thirteen hundred feet across the river. The falls look spectacular when you pull your car off the highway and walk over to the scenic overlook, but it is even more so when you are in a boat in the river just below the falls, the churning water, turgid and restless. Seated in the boat you peek out from under the brim of your hat and look upriver toward the falls—there where the river slides along its rocky bottom and then suddenly goes ass-over-teakettle as it drops out of its channel into somewhere far below—a deafening admixture of water, air, spray, and foam. The tumbling water traps the air in the water and creates millions of bubbles. In turn, the trapped air in those bubbles refracts light and colors the falls white. Down in the plunge pool, the bubbles explode and the river is no longer white, save for the foam lines where the current hurries its way along, the whirlpools and eddies sucking their way downstream between the hemmed-in banks.

While I usually fish with fly-fishing gear, such is not the case with salmon fishing, at least not on the Willamette, so I have had an uphill journey on my way to becoming a salmon fisherman. Fortunately, a couple of friends have invited me to fish on their salmon boats and they have helped me learn the ropes, or more precisely, how to rig-up the appropriate tackle. I eventually learned to rig-up cut-plug herring baits as I beheaded those baitfish at just the right angle of the knife and then threaded a pair of 3/0 hooks and the twenty-five-pound leader through the little fish. I learned how to rig-up the terminal tackle with Duolock snap swivels, green and red beads, flashers, and spinners. I learned to use elastic string and tie tiny sardine fillets around plastic lures. I learned when to select the appropriate cannonball weights from four ounces to twelve ounces and how to carefully put the entire assemblage overboard without snarling up the gear. I put rubber gloves on when putting the bait on so as to mask my scent. The whole process was a far cry from tying an improved clinch knot on a size-16 Blue-Winged Olive dun with a 6X tippet.

The contrast between fly fishing and salmon fishing is a mile wide. For example, not too long ago I was fly-fishing for trout at East Lake. I was trying to tie on a small *Callibaetis* emerger using a 6X tippet. Younger anglers may not have a problem with that, but older folks will instantly understand what I mean, especially if the light is dim, your fingers are cold, and the boat is rocking back and forth with a wind blowing across the lake.

Cut to a week later and I was in my garage trying to tie on large Duolock snap swivels on each end of a short length of stout leader. The leader was to be attached from the main line to a flasher. While a 6X tip-pet is almost invisible, a sixty-pound leader is very much there—actually too much there because it was difficult to tighten the knot on such a thick piece of leader. I put a leather glove on one hand and put the knotted snap swivel on a big hook on one of the rafters in my garage. Then I pulled down hard on the leader and tightened the knot.

I purchased my own salmon rod, level-line reel, and tackle so I could tag along with those salmon-fishing veterans. I was happy to be the bait boy and first mate, ready to help the boat slide off the trailer and later operate the trolling motor when the captain wanted to take a break. I have been familiar with small boats for years and own a drift boat myself, so when I take it along, it is my responsibility. So as first mate, it was nice *not* to be the one in charge. I have been especially happy as first mate on our salmon-fishing trips because someone other than me has to navigate through the urban boating traffic below the falls.

One day my friend Alan and I launched his boat and ventured upriver almost all the way to the falls. It was late in the spring Chinook run, at the end of May, but the fish were still holding—waiting for another surge up toward their spawning waters. Alan deftly weaved his boat through the other boats—some trolling upriver and others downriver. The river is quite narrow in some places. At some of the well-known salmon holes, boats anchor right next to one another creating what is called a hog line. You find a slot here and there where you can slip through that line of boats—and we did.

I looked out at today's power boats, graphite rods, and line-counter reels and thought about what it must have looked like one hundred years ago when those fishermen were using their wooden rowboats. And one hundred years before that, the fishermen on the Willamette were from the Clackamas tribe or maybe the Clowewalla tribe: They stood on their wooden platforms as their long-handled hoop nets cut into the swirling water. Hoisting up a thrashing thirty-pound fish onto a small, spray-splattered wooden platform would have been no easy task. Those native fishermen lived in a village named Walamt, and it was right across the river from where we were weaving our way through the tangle of fiberglass and aluminum boats.

Tragically, by the time the homesteading pioneers came along, most of those Indians had already died due to malarial and smallpox epidemics. Afterwards the remaining Indians and other fishers came along with nets, fish wheels, and rod and reel. Other pioneers began to put the falls to work: The magic of falling water and gravity powered a lumber mill, paper mill, woolen mill, and by 1888 one of the nation's first hydroelectric plants. All the while the salmon continued their migration every spring, deaf to the humming noise of the power lines that soon electrified the youthful city of Portland. In the next century more than two dozen dams were harnessed for hydropower and flood control, and as a result, many of those dams blocked off hundreds of miles of spawning salmon and steelhead streams. Today the Willamette Valley comprises 70 percent of the state's population, including much of the state's industry and agriculture. While the salmon have soldiered on, their population has been sharply reduced due to the usual consequences of industrial and agricultural development, as well as the dams. Though hatcheries have helped to supplement the wild fish, there have been adverse consequences with that, too. While a ghost of the past, still an estimated fifty thousand spring Chinook run up the Willamette every year. The wild fish must be released, but hatchery-reared fish can be boated when the season allows.

On that day in late May when we were motoring up toward the falls, the season was indeed open and we were hoping to put a hatchery fish or two in the boat. We slowly went upstream under the tall Interstate 205 bridge. Our offerings trailed through the dark water behind the boat: Sometimes we used cut-plug herring; other times we used colorful spinners; and still at other times we used big gaudy plastic flatfish lures. My bright flasher and cannonball were spread out in the cold, hurly-burly current. Some three to four feet of leader below the flasher was a bright-gold spinner attached to a stout sharp single hook. The weight of the tackle and the steady troll of the outboard caused the rod to bend in a graceful bow, its fine tip telegraphing the rhythmic movement through the current, its cork handle secure in the starboard rod holder. I had tightened up the drag so I could just barely pull the line off the spool. I clicked a button on the side of the reel, so if the line started to run off the spool, I would be able to hear it.

With the tackle overboard and trolling through the cold water, I thought of the fish below, under the surface, finning their way toward the falls, looking at all manner of bright things wobbling about in the current. I imagined that those Chinook might have been grouchy, displeased by the hubbub in the darkened, once-quiet water.

What is this charade? What is with all those gaudy things, spinning and thumping and buzzing through the water? And why are all those headless herring swimming around?

I looked over at my neighbor in his boat and his rod tip was but a few feet from mine. It was the same on the port side where Alan's rod tip was only a few feet away from a forest of rods in a guided operation with six clients onboard. I do not know how the guides do not get snarled with all that gear trolling through the water. When fly-fishing for nymphs using split-shot and two flies you can get into an awful mess. But in a salmon boat with half-pound weights, foot-long flashers, hooks, bead chains, and long heavy leaders, a snarl can get very nasty—the line twisting into an unholy tightened braid. More than often you simply unsheathe your knife and start all over again.

In some places the river broadened and the boats were not as close to one another, so I was able to steer the boat while Alan wanted to change his tackle. He pried open a hollow lure and put a sardine fillet inside it, and then he rubbed some bloody tuna scent liquid on the lure, too. Salmon are very sensitive to scent. Local outdoor stores display rows of bottles of various scents with the aroma of garlic, herring, anchovy, shrimp, sardine, or tuna.

As we trolled upriver toward the falls, the massive abandoned paper mill on the river had a post-apocalyptic feel, the paint peeling, the steel structures rusted and dirty. The men working at the mill with their hard-hats on their heads were long gone: No one was on the catwalks or on roadways where forklifts once skittered about. The riverbanks were an unpeopled canyon of concrete and steel, the water below deep and ominous. I would not want to jump in. I saw a young man on a paddleboard moving by and I thought that was not a good thing to do. Not only was the current treacherous, but sea lions were lurking about. The past few years more and more sea lions have gone across the bar at the Columbia

River swimming upriver more than one hundred miles to feed on salmon at the base of the falls. Those dark brown pinnipeds measure up to seven feet long and can weigh as much as eight hundred pounds, so hitting one of them on a paddleboard could be dangerous.

Some salmon fishermen use kayaks on the Willamette, and they too pay close attention to the sea lions. A friend of mine fishes out of a Hobie, a pedal-driven type of kayak. He once had a salmon on his line and a sea lion grabbed the fish. He understood who was in charge and soon his tackle was long gone. Another time Alan and I saw a sea lion catch a salmon some sixty yards off our stern. The lion was thrashing about on the surface trying to devour the wiggling fish. Suddenly, a bald eagle swooped down and tried to grab the fish out of the lion's mouth. A marvelous fight commenced, and not surprisingly, the eagle did not win.

Up close to the concrete wall on the east side of the river, we saw an angler catch a fish. The men in their boat netted it and congratulated one another. We were close by and gave them a thumbs-up.

"Fine fish!" I yelled out across the water at the happy fisherman.

Maybe we were in the zone. I hoped so. We continued moving upriver to where the boats were lined up at the fishing deadline below the falls. There the river roared across the rocky ridge, becoming a river of white, thundering, the spray rising into a veil of mist. It was a sunny day, the blue sky brushed by the wispy cirrus clouds high above the river. In the old days the Indians set up their platforms on those very rocky banks and dipped their nets into the roiling water. The salmon, then and now, move their powerful tails, sprint through the fast water, and then jump wildly in the wetted air. Sometimes they fall back into the flow and try again. At other times they slip over the top of a rocky ledge and rest in a hidden declivity for the next ascension.

Near the deadline we turned around and began trolling back down-river, the foam bubbling up from the turbulent water. In most places there was a pattern to the trolling so we and the other boats fell into line, so while there were many boats on the water, it was not helter-skelter. Over the past few hours, we had seen very few other boaters with fish on. There did not appear to be much of a bite. However, we saw a sea lion roll every now and again—its ample blubbered body immune to the cold river water—so we assumed that the fish must still be there because where there are sea lions around there must be fish.

As we trolled back downriver under the Interstate 205 bridge, I got a sharp, strong pull on the rod. I stood up and took the rod out of the holder. The rod was deeply bowed and throbbing. Alan reeled in his line, but it took a while. We were surrounded by other boats, and it was not easy for him to reel in his line and steer at the same time. While a flat-water river here, it has a strong current so somebody has to keep his or her hand on the tiller or the boat would veer off toward the bank or bang into another boat.

All the while *my* Chinook did its best to pull away from that sharp object that was stuck in its jaw. Why it opened its mouth and snapped at my gold spinner with red beads we will never know. Fishing for salmon in freshwater is always difficult because they are on their way to find their natal waters, spawn, and die. Their body fat allows them to sustain their journey, and so generally, they are not interested in eating. They are a tight-lipped bunch, and that is why it is always tough to persuade them to open their mouths. Fishing with flies, by comparison, is easy because the fish want to eat—every day. All you have to figure out is what type of food the fish are taking at the moment. Obviously, that is easier said than done. My bookshelves are bowed down with the weight of dozens of fly-fishing books targeting how, when, and where to "match the hatch."

But this Chinook did open its mouth—for whatever reason. It probably tried to spit it out as soon as it felt the unnatural sensation of a steel spinner rubbing up against the inside of its mouth. But it was too late. The fish was hooked and so was I—in my own way—thrilled after many hours of waiting.

"Oh, it's a strong one!" I told Alan.

I could not see the fish in the dark water, though I was doing my best to crank up the line, inch by inch. Chinook generally prefer deeper water and do not often jump compared to steelhead. I reeled in the line a bit more and by then Alan's gear was stowed away and he was able to steer away from the other boats and find some open water where we could fight the fish without interference. But there still could be plenty of interference as I nervously kept a sharp eye out for sea lions. Oftentimes *they* keep a sharp eye on the anglers, too, and when they notice a commotion in the boat and see the net flash, they know that dinner is on the way. The year before Alan had a fish on and a sea lion chomped off a good portion of the fish before he could get it to the boat. I did not want that to happen. The mainline and leader were both heavy, so I could safely push down hard on the star drag. I would have liked to have played the fish longer, but time is not on your side when there are sea lions about.

However, I did not want to bring the fish in too quickly either or it might slam into the side of the boat and flip the hook out of its mouth. I wanted to tire the fish a bit so it would not make trouble at the boat. Alan had the net at hand, but I wanted him to hold off until I could lead the fish by its head. Suddenly, I could see the chrome silver color of the salmon's flanks and its dark top. It looked mean and likely it did not care for me at all. While I feel almost reverential about salmon and steelhead, I imagined that the fish did not feel the same way—after all, I was doing my best to try to kill it.

I got in close to the fish and I could see that the adipose fin had been clipped. That cranked up the tension in the boat. If the fish was wild, we would have had to release it anyhow. But now that it was a hatchery fish, I wanted that salmon dinner, fresh from the Pacific where it had fed on anchovies or herring a few months earlier.

The fish saw the boat and darted away.

"That's okay," I said to myself.

The fish did not run out much line and I brought it back toward the boat again. I stepped back a bit and lifted the rod and gently pulled the fish, head first, closer to the side of the boat. Alan thrust the net downward into the water and the fish swam right into it. In a nanosecond the thrashing fish was out of the water and onto the floor of the boat.

"We got it!" I said.

I knelt down, found the billy club, and penned the fish down, wiggly and slippery as it was. The brilliant silver-colored Chinook did not have much time left to live ... I paused ... and then I raised the club upward.

Whack!

Down came the club onto the fish's skull. Then I hit it again. The fish twitched about and soon what was once full of life was lifeless. I grabbed my camera and took a picture of the salmon and the shiny spinner that still was hooked in its lower left jaw. I took the spinner out, got out my knife, and cut into the gills to bleed it.

We congratulated one another because such fishing is a group effort, with the pilot, the netter, and the angler all participating. Before long I dressed out the fish: It was a fat one but not a large one, about ten pounds. In the old days those spring Chinook sometimes weighed in at over thirty pounds.

I tossed the innards out onto the water, right across from where the native Walamt village once was some three hundred years ago, or maybe seven hundred years ago. I am sure those fishmongers knew exactly how to utilize their fish.

My way of utilizing the fish would involve slicing off the lateral fins. Then after filleting it I would toss out the backbone and head, remove the pin bones with a pair of needle-nose pliers, dust a bit of lemon pepper onto the glistening, firm orange-pink flesh, and put the fillet on the grill. And as the salmon aroma invisibly whiffed its way into the air, I would think about the first moment when I saw that silver flash in the dark waters far below the interstate bridge, at the end of the Oregon Trail.

Chapter Seven

A Boy and His River

The Willamette, the Sandy, the Klickitat, the Deschutes, the John Day—those and many other rivers flow into the Columbia, the Great River of the West. But what about the Columbia itself: its terrain, its people, its fishery, its alterations, its past, its future?

The Columbia is a bundle of contradictions. In places, such as the Columbia River Gorge National Scenic Area, it is as picturesque as can be with many waterfalls and a broad and strong river cutting through the steep, forested mountains. Farther to the east, the river is not as scenic with its slack-water reservoirs and a parched landscape of stunted sagebrush and rock. The river's shoreline is old and new at once with an operating nuclear power plant along its banks in eastern Washington state. A few miles downstream, one of North America's oldest human remains is the nine-thousand-year-old Kennewick Man whose skeleton was discovered along the banks of the river in 1996 a few miles away from where I grew up in the town of Richland. While he and his people had lived there for millennia, the river was one of the last large rivers to be discovered by Europeans and Americans during the Age of Discovery.

My first memories of the Columbia are of tumbleweeds and sagebrush, a waterless land save a blue ribbon of running water flowing down from the glaciated Canadian Rockies, winding across the basalt flats. The 1,240-mile Columbia River drains an area the size of France. Its watershed includes major portions of Oregon, Washington, Idaho, and Montana, smaller portions of Wyoming, Utah, and Nevada, and much of southeastern British Columbia. The Columbia rushes out into the Pacific

Ocean with a discharge of more than a million cubic feet of water every four seconds. By volume it is the third-largest river in the Lower 48, exceeded only by the Ohio and Mississippi Rivers.

Along the middle section of the Columbia where I grew up were groves of cottonwood trees and willows, and along the shoreline there was a border of damp mud smelling of ripe organisms, rotting and fertile at once. Outside of the city of Richland and away from the river's edge, the countryside was thick with beige-colored cheatgrass—the barbed seed pods that stick to your socks when you walk through the open fields. The tallest vegetation around was sagebrush, which can grow to be as tall as a tall man in some places, but on the whole measure a yard high. The pungent smell of the gray-green sage leaves drifted across the terrain where the land rises away from the river to the treeless Horse Heaven Hills, where the Earth stretches its rumpled skin. The summers were hot and the sunsets were streaked with wispy clouds colored minute by minute from pink to crimson to violet; and high overhead a once dainty blue sky darkened slowly into navy and finally into a moonless blackness spangled with stars.

The Columbia River where I grew up was not like the mouth at Astoria that is nearly five miles across, but it was not a headwater river either. It was an in-between river, much too big to swim across, but too small for commercial barges and tugs to navigate. I can dimly remember that my river once was a free-flowing river throughout our whole area, including the Umatilla Rapids where the river turned the corner going from south to west. By the time I was in second grade, the McNary Dam was completed, and it inundated those rapids for good and created a reservoir all the way up to our city. Just upstream of our city, the river once again started to become a real river with a swift current, gravel bars, and islands. That part of the river is the longest free-flowing stretch of the Columbia River in the United States above the reach of tide, and it is called the Hanford Reach National Monument. Farther north the river also runs freely for a few miles from the upper end of Grand Coulee Dam's reservoir to the US-Canadian border. The Hanford Reach has islands upon islands, some large, others not so large. Downriver of Richland there are few islands, just one long, wide languid body of water, what the US Corps of Engineers refers to as a lake. I call it a reservoir. Some would say that a river without islands is an emasculated river, one without soul, tamed by rebar and concrete. Others might say that a harnessed river, like the Columbia, is a friendly and helpful river, one that stays floods, generates hydroelectricity, and irrigates the dry land by turning the omnipresent sagebrush terrain into green fields of corn and grapes and alfalfa.

As a boy, I was ignorant about what kind of river my river was, and I did not notice how it changed year by year as one dam after the next was completed until only the Reach remained unfettered. I did not know that the river had become a working river, an electric river, a potato river. I did not realize that the dams brought inexpensive hydroelectricity to our home. The desert bloomed with federally subsidized irrigation river water. Meanwhile, the estimated ten to sixteen million salmon that historically once migrated up the Columbia and Snake Rivers every year has dwindled to a small fraction today, in large part because the dams blocked half of the salmon's spawning and rearing habitat and also because of the ongoing deleterious operations of the dams. It is no wonder that many of those salmon and steelhead populations are listed under the federal Endangered Species Act.

As a boy, I did not know about any of that because a child cannot be expected to plumb the depths: "You cannot get water from a deep well with a short rope," says an old Chinese proverb.

As a boy, I considered the Columbia was my friend: It had its hazards, to be sure, but with a few precautions a boy and a river could have a lifelong friendship. The river flowed by our banks day and night, season in and season out, and all the while my life moved along, too. Rivers and time are intertwined, one tangible and the other ethereal. The river's current flows by as do we. A river seems the same when you look at it day in and day out, but its permanence is deceptive because it is always moving, just as we are always moving through time. The water in the river today is not the same water that flowed by yesterday or will flow by tomorrow.

As a boy, I thought of the fish as part of the river and the river as part of the fish. Fish are surrounded by water day and night just as we are surrounded by land and air. Fish "know," in their own way, that a riffle is where nymphs get dislodged from the rocky bottom and are swept away with the current. In turn the fish know where they station themselves in their respective feeding lanes. The fish know that a pool is where they like to lollygag, not a care in the world, safe in the deep water, lazy, the current nonexistent. The telltale foam lines also are where the bugs collect in the conflicting currents, where the fish queue up for dinner. A river is life to a fish, its nutrients, its life-giving oxygen, and when a river shallows out in the summer, the fish knowingly drift downstream and seek out the dark holes under the cutbanks.

A boy enters this water-world deftly and mysteriously when he goes fishing. Maybe he wades up to his knees to get a good cast out into an eddy. Maybe he stumbles and falls into the water. But he is able-bodied and crafty and gets back on his feet quickly, dripping wet but safe and sound. Before long he and the river and the fish intermingle. Sometimes it is hard to tell if the river absorbs the boy or if the boy absorbs the river. The two are intertwined and the longer the boy wades and fishes and swims in the river, the more he becomes part of it: To a boy, a river is his best friend. If he is lucky, he may find himself on the water in all types of boats, for there is nothing quite as fun as being in a boat on a river, especially when a boy is finally able to pilot a boat and not just be a passenger.

The Columbia is a large river and has seen many different types of boats on its waters, from prehistoric canoes to sailing ships, sternwheelers, cabin cruisers, and behemoth ocean-going freighters. The first large European ships that plied the waters of the Columbia were tall-masted sailing ships. While the estuary of the Columbia is some five miles wide, oddly those early mariners failed to discover the Columbia, even though for centuries the Western world was searching for the mysterious River of the West. The failure to discover the Columbia was especially noteworthy because the mouth of the Columbia is not a delta like the Mississippi River whereby a large river can braid into many channels and dissipate the river's flow. In such rivers it can be difficult to locate the mouth. In contrast, the Columbia has virtually no delta. Every second it discharges 265,000 cubic feet of freshwater straight into the ocean. It is like a gigantic pipe gushing into the saltwater day and night. When this onslaught of freshwater hits the ocean tides at the entrance of the river, the turbulent, crashing breakers become as rough as any bar in the world.

As a boy, I knew little about the explorers who discovered the Great River of the West. Of course, the very nature of "discovering" the river is an ethnocentric point of view since the Chinook Indians and other tribes at the mouth of the Columbia had already discovered the river centuries before. All the same, the Age of Discovery—sparked by Columbus, Magellan, and others—was a momentous time in history, a time when the Europeans and later the Americans first mapped the entire globe. One of the last places of discovery was the Pacific Northwest, because most of it was a blank spot on the map until the early nineteenth century.

Only much later did I learn about those who explored the North Pacific coast, and one of the first was Sir Francis Drake. He and his ship, the *Golden Hind*, sailed as far north as Vancouver Island in 1579 and did not notice the mouth of the Columbia. Some twenty-four years later in 1603, a Spanish ship captain named Martin de Aguilar first sighted the Oregon coast. It is unclear how far he and his ship sailed north, but at any rate he did not mention the Columbia.

Another Spanish captain, Juan Perez, sailed north toward the Columbia on his way up the coast in 1774, but he did not notice the Columbia River. A year later yet another Spanish captain, Bruno Heceta in his ship the *Santiago*, sailed up the West Coast and noticed there was a large estuary off the coast a few hundred miles north of California. He speculated that there might be a large river there. He noted the capes on either side of the estuary, but he did not attempt to cross the bar. He plotted the latitude on his chart. Unknowingly, he had discovered the entrance of the Columbia.

Two years later Captain James Cook sailed east and north from Hawaii and sighted the Oregon coast in 1778. His expedition sailed as far north as the Bering Sea, but he did not notice the mouth of the Columbia. Ten years later a fur-trading captain named John Meares sailed up the Oregon coast. By then Captain Heceta had pinpointed the estuary in question on the navigation charts. Meares located the proper latitude on the estuary. He tried to cross the bar but was unsuccessful and therefore concluded that there was no river there.

In 1791 an American fur-trading captain named Robert Gray spent nine days trying to cross the bar and was still unsuccessful. The next year in April 1792, he met up with a British captain named George Vancouver just inside the entrance of the Strait of Juan de Fuca. Gray told Vancouver that he had not been able to cross the bar at the estuary in question. Vancouver told Gray that he had seen the same estuary. One of Vancouver's exploratory missions was to seek the fabled Northwest Passage linking the Atlantic and Pacific Oceans. Vancouver speculated that such a passage would be much larger than the estuary that he had observed, and consequently, he felt that the estuary was not particularly noteworthy so he had continued on up the coast. The two ships, one American and the other British, left the Strait of Juan de Fuca, Vancouver sailing north and Gray sailing south.

A month later Gray again was back at the mouth of the Columbia and tried to cross the bar and failed. But he did not give up. Finally, on May 11, 1792, Gray's ship, the *Columbia Rediviva*, crossed the bar and he found that his ship was suddenly in a large river. Over the next few weeks, the expedition penetrated some thirty-five miles upriver. With their logs and observations, they were able to prove that they had, in fact, discovered the great River of the West and they named the river after their ship.

Meanwhile Captain Vancouver was still exploring and mapping the British Columbia coast. In October of 1792 he met up with a Spanish commander at Nootka Sound on the west side of Vancouver Island. The commander told Vancouver of Gray's Columbia River discovery. Vancouver apparently was not pleased. Another one of Vancouver's missions on that multi-year exploratory voyage was to find whether or not there were major rivers flowing into the Pacific Ocean. He meticulously charted much of the area from Oregon to northern British Columbia, month after month, year after year. His mission was trying, exhausting, and dangerous. One can only imagine how exasperated Vancouver must have been when he learned that someone else—in fact, another nation—had now discovered the River of the West.

Vancouver immediately sailed south from Nootka Sound and soon found himself at the mysterious estuary. His large ship, *The Discovery*, was unable to cross the bar, but a smaller vessel aboard the ship was able to cross. The expedition eventually utilized an even smaller vessel, a longboat, and Vancouver's second in command, Lieutenant William Broughton, proceeded 120 miles upriver from the mouth, just east of present-day Portland. Vancouver named a number of landmarks on this voyage, such as Mount Hood, but the discovery of the Columbia was not to be his. After he returned to England, he had to tell the Admiralty that another nation, a fledgling one at that, had discovered the great River of the West. And to make matters worse, he had to tell his superiors that, unfortunately, there was no such Northwest Passage.

Gray's discovery of the Columbia helped the United States push the nation's boundary northward from the Columbia River to the 49th parallel during the negotiations of the Treaty of Oregon in 1846. We will never know, but if Vancouver had discovered the Columbia instead of Gray, perhaps the area north of the Columbia River would be part of Canada today.

I have always liked to see the headwaters of rivers, as well as where they flowed into the salt. I think my father had the same longing, because one summer vacation our family traveled to the headwaters of the Columbia. Those headwaters were discovered in 1807 by a British-Canadian fur trader and surveyor named David Thompson working with the North West Company. The source of the river is a shallow, eight-mile-long lake appropriately named Columbia Lake, hard up against the western slope of the Canadian Rockies. A village called Canal Flats is on the banks of the lake. The outlet of the lake is the beginning of the river, and it flows 470 miles through British Columbia down to the US border.

Just south of the border is Grand Coulee Dam's 150-mile-long reservoir. A great deal of that water is pumped out of the reservoir and into miles of canals. After the dam was completed in the 1940s, the desert bloomed with one thousand square miles of corn, grapes, potatoes, and alfalfa fields. The runoff from this irrigated water flowed downward into various impoundments, such as the Potholes Reservoir. Even as a boy, I understood that where there is water there are fish. The river's water had been captured in an unusual way, but it was Columbia River water. And in the early season before the summer got too hot, my father and I traveled north and fished for rainbow trout in those pothole lakes.

Our tackle did not include fly-fishing gear back then. I never saw any anglers using flies back in the day on the Columbia or on the nearby seep lakes. Nowadays many Columbia basin tributaries have excellent blue-ribbon fly-fishing fisheries for trout and steelhead, such as the Deschutes, Metolius, Yakima, Clearwater, Henry's Fork, Blackfoot, and Grande Ronde, but the Columbia itself still has never been known as a fly-fishing river. Most of the way, at least up to the Canadian border, the river is too big to easily fish with flies, with some exceptions. At any rate I have never fished with flies on the Columbia itself; instead, I have utilized other tackle to catch salmon, steelhead, perch, and smallmouth bass, but not flies. Maybe sometime I will rig-up my fly outfit and get to work. I am told that a number of fly anglers fish the seep lakes in the basin. In the Reach there must be some good fly angling, too, with those broad riffles and alluring back eddies. And up near the Canadian border, where the river runs free again for a few miles, there are fine large resident trout ready to be hooked . . . maybe next month, maybe next year, maybe in another lifetime . . . we'll see.

With our spin gear in the back of the car, Dad drove the Pontiac station wagon down a dead-end dirt road where we were to fish at one of the pothole lakes. The desert evening air was cold and sharp, the stars sparkling achingly close, the city lights far, far away. The moon was AWOL and the clouds, too, were on vacation. Our camp was rudimentary. I cannot recall if we fired up the Coleman stove to cook dinner or maybe we just ate some cold cuts. And I cannot recall either if we made a small warming fire or not. But I do recall that we lugged our ice cooler out onto the ground and set out our rods and tackle up against a nearby sagebrush. We folded down the back seat of the Pontiac wagon and blew up two air mattresses and that was our tent.

"Goodnight, Tommy," Dad said.

"Goodnight, Dad," I replied as I snuggled into the sleeping bag.

Overhead the firmament was black save for the dusted galaxies sprinkled across the darkness. As a boy, I found the stars wondrous and at the same time nihilistic for the night sky is too large, our accomplishments puny beyond measure, the blackness of the sky less black than empty, vacuous, stretching from horizon to horizon without meaning or purpose. Compared to the comforts of home, a nighttime treeless camp can be at once overwhelming—and also exciting to a boy.

At first light my father and I both reluctantly climbed out of our warm sleeping bags, shivered as we dressed, went about our business dutifully, gathered up our rods and tackle, food, and canteens, and hiked down the trail to the water. Before us was one of the little potholes, its waters hopefully enlivened with trout. We scampered down the crumbling rust-brown columnar basalt—postpiles as they are called. We found a small spit that reached out into the lake. From there we could cast our lures out over a wide area. The water was not shallow, but it did not appear to be terribly deep either—good fishing water. Dad, with his curly red-brown hair and brown eyes, had his rod and reel rigged up quickly and so did I. I tied on a barrel swivel with an improved clinch knot and then I put on a homemade red-and-white Dardevle spoon. I purchased a dozen of those spoons from Herter's Co., a mail-order outdoor company. I also ordered split rings, barrel swivels, and hooks. The spoons were silver-bright and I used some of them as is, but I painted most of them.

The spoon splashed out onto the placid surface of the water, the concentric circles rippling, the water ruffled in the calmness of the morning. I waited for a few seconds while the spoon descended toward the bottom. Then I reeled in the spoon with a medium retrieval rate. The spoon was a thick one so I did not need a spit-shot for weight. Dad used much the same setup with his spinning rod and reel, and we worked in tandem casting out into different directions so we would not cross our lines. I adjusted the rate of the retrieval as I went along and so did he.

We fished all morning and caught a number of nice early-season trout measuring up to thirteen inches or so. I released some of the smaller fish and clubbed the large ones using a nearby rock. I slipped the dead fish on a stringer and placed them in the shallow water, the fish stunningly bright, silvery with a faint pink lateral line. The sun slowly rose across the broad sky, the terrain flat save a rimrock castellation off in the distance.

By noon we had our limit and we both shared in the cleaning operation. I always liked the feel of the slick, slippery fish on my hands and the sharp blade of my jackknife in my hand that opened up the fish's white underbelly. Dad always reminded me to make sure to run my thumb down along the fish's spine taking all the blood away. The second most important part of cleaning a fish properly was to discard all the blood-rich gills. We did not want coagulated blood on the fish's flesh.

I broke off some tall grasses and wetted them down with water and put them into the creel. Then I put the fish in the creel and slung it over my shoulder. Later we put the fish on a block of ice in the cooler. And after we returned home we had a trout feed: the flour-dusted headless fish sizzling in hot oil. With the season still early in the year, the flesh was faintly pink and flavorful. I peeled the soft, flaked meat off the backbone and savored the mild and subtle flavor of fresh trout.

The water in our little pothole lake was composed of Columbia River water, water that had once been siphoned off near the Canadian border. Some of that Columbia River water seeped into the potholes, some of it migrated even farther down the slope—sometimes as surface water, sometimes under the ground—and some of that water eventually returned to the river's channel. Day in and day out, the river flowed by, past the town of Mattawa, past Beverly and Vernita, with the river forever churning and gurgling along. The river's current itself kept pace with the slope of the river's bottom: the flatter the slope the slower the current and vice versa. Interestingly, a river's flow takes place not only from the bottom up but also from the bottom down, because there is no real bottom to a river. Beneath the boulders, gravel, and sand is the hyporheic zone, the basement as it were, where the sub-surface water in the porous sediments and the surface water intermix. Gravity sends these waters ever downward, sometimes percolating into the earth, sometimes flowing back into the river. I have seen more than one stream that was barren in one stretch and well watered in another.

A river's water is always on the move, as are we. Even still waters, such as lakes and ponds, have movement, but their movements are more subtle than are rivers. Lakes have thermal currents, wind-whipped currents, inlets and outlets. A river's components are more dynamic, but despite the complexities of a river, they entail three simple ingredients: water, terrain, and gravity. And while elemental, those building blocks create a river of complexity, for a natural river is never straight: It tumbles down from mountains filled with rapids, later with meanders and oxbows and braids. And the threads of the river's current weave back and forth, side by side and up and down, melded into whole cloth, a world that fish are accustomed to but in which we, awkward as we are in the water, are next to helpless. Like an eagle that senses the many air currents in the sky, so a fish senses the many watery currents in a river's flow.

As a boy, I somehow dimly knew that a river is complicated, especially a large river. If I had grown up on the banks of a smaller river, it might have been different. But a large river is endlessly complex. Still, to a boy, a river is basically a playground. As I got older, it was more than that. It dawned on me eventually—maybe even subliminally—that a river is both passive and active, nature's dichotomy. I witnessed its activity year in and year out, its floods, currents, whirlpools, rapids, riffles, and eddies. A big river can be overwhelming, lethal at times. I also witnessed the river's passivity as massive concrete dams marched their way up the Columbia and Snake Rivers. By the mid-1970s the river finally had been stilled. It is said that water does not fear fire, and that may be true, but it met its match with concrete and rebar. The active Columbia, the wild one running between its banks with vigor and aplomb, still exists in a few places, such as the Reach. There the river chatters merrily across the broad gravel bars and rushes by as it flows around an island and then stitches the current threads back together downstream.

Lower downriver below the last of the dams where the tides begin to affect the river's current, there, there at last, the river flows freely once again. While there are no riffles or rapids in that 140-mile, tidal-borne lower river, nonetheless it has a robust current with huge eddies and whirlpools: The pulse of the river beats with a sedulous rhythm, the current bursting itself to get to the sea. The closer to the mouth, the stronger is the tidal flow, and by the time the two waters join—the saltwater tides and the freshwater river current—the river is miles wide and violent, anything but a playground. To the ship captains seeking to cross the bar—from the Spanish explorers to today's salmon fishermen and massive freighters—the river is not always a friend.

Section II
Rainforest Rivers

CHAPTER EIGHT

A Fish of a Thousand Casts

THE COLUMBIA RIVER AND ITS TRIBUTARIES COULD EASILY COMPRISE the entirety of this book, but it is time to move on because there are too many other wonderful western rivers beyond the Columbia basin. On either side of the mouth of the Columbia, there are many rivers that flow down out of the coastal mountains and empty directly into the Pacific Ocean. Most of those coastal rivers are short, mostly less than one hundred miles long, but their combined discharge is immense because of the sodden North Pacific coast. From northern California to the Olympic Peninsula, the prevailing southwesterlies push the moist Pacific air into higher and higher elevations where it is subjected to less pressure, expands, and cools. As it cools, water vapor in the air condenses into water droplets that form clouds, and when those clouds reach their saturation point, it rains.

And rain it does: the ground soggy underfoot, saplings sprouting from nurse logs, fungi, spike moss, tall evergreens everywhere, alders and vine maples, multi-canopies and an undergrowth tangle of green, some rooted in the earth, others not, such as the epiphytes, plants that do not grow out of the soil but instead grow on other plants, such as ferns, mosses, and lichens. At the northwest corner of the Lower 48 is the Quillayute weather station, which records an average of just over one hundred inches of rain annually. At the summit of the Olympic Mountains, the annual precipitation can nearly double that amount. By the time the clouds slip over the crest, they are wrung out and the east side of the peninsula lies in a rain shadow with precipitation measuring only twenty inches a year in places. To the south, the rain continues. The Lewis and Clark Expedition wintered at the mouth of the Columbia in 1805–06. In the 106 days they spent at Fort Clatsop, they recorded ninety-four days of rain. Apparently, a number of the men wished they were back at the previous year's winter encampment in the Mandan Village in North Dakota, despite the sub-freezing temperatures there. The southern Oregon and northern California coast is a bit drier than to the north, but still it rains sixty to eighty inches a year there.

The deluge of rain and snowmelt on the west slope of the Pacific coast must go somewhere, and as the alert angler knows, it goes into rivers. The rivers are many, from the Sol Duc at the north end of the Olympic Peninsula to the Hoh, Queets, Quinault, and others. To the south in Oregon are many coastal rivers, such as the Wilson, Trask, Nehalem, Nestucca, Alsea, Rogue, and Chetco. Still farther south are the northern California coastal rivers, including the Klamath, Smith, Mad, Eel, Van Duzen, and Russian.

It is difficult to comprehend the volume of those coastal rivers. The Queets, for example, is a fifty-mile-long river that flows out of the Humes Glacier on the southeast flanks of Mount Olympus. The flow varies dramatically due to the season as there are no dams. The average discharge of the Queets at its mouth is forty-three hundred cubic feet per second. In contrast, the discharge at the mouth of the San Juan River, a major tributary of the Colorado River, is about half that. The Queets has a basin equivalent to that of the city of Tulsa, Oklahoma. The San Juan has a basin equivalent to that of West Virginia. And the Queets is not unusual on the Olympics' West End rivers. Just south of the Queets is the Quinault and just to the north is the Hoh, all short on distance but big on flow because the western side of the Olympic Peninsula is the wettest area in the contiguous United States.

While the Olympics were discovered by the Europeans and Americans several hundred years ago, it took many more years for anyone to actually penetrate the interior of that rugged rainforest. As the crow flies, the distance between the crest of the Olympics and the Pacific Ocean is less than fifty miles. But on foot the distance was an entirely different matter as people had to encounter glaciers, alpine mountain ridges, canyons, and dense rainforests where the sun is a stranger, where the western hemlock and Sitka spruce rise up to 250 feet in height and measure up to sixty feet in circumference. The Press Expedition explored the interior for the first time in 1890. It took them months to traverse the peninsula, and the five men involved nearly starved to death in the process.

The Olympic beach itself has had a troubled past, too. In 1775 Captain Juan de la Bodega y Quadra sent a party of men from his ship to the mouth of the Hoh to get freshwater, and they were killed by Indians. Twelve years later another group of seamen from Captain William Barkley's East India Company ship met the same fate at the mouth of the Hoh.

My brothers and I once hiked down the lower Hoh, and when we got to the mouth, we saw some Indians on the other side where the Hoh Indian Reservation is located. They waved at us and we waved back. One man yelled out at us about something from across the river. With the wind and the roar of the surf, we could not hear what he said, but it did not appear that he and his friends were hostile. We uncapped our water bottles, sat down, and enjoyed the view of the Hoh flowing out of the Olympic National Park, its headwaters from the Hoh Glacier on the flanks of Mount Olympus, its turquoise-tinged water, cold and clean, rippling all the way down the broad gravel riverbed with its millions of smooth gray stones, its sun-bleached driftwood logs stuck in the sand, its current vanquished where it meets its match, where the ebb tide sucks the river water far out into the boundless sea. Later, somewhere out in the vastness of the ocean, the sun will warm the surface and cause the ocean's skin to evaporate and become water vapor, and later it will condense into clouds and they will drift in toward the mountains and rain upon the land and that runoff will—

"Time to go back?" Richard asked me.

"Sure," I said, my reverie gone. I stood up, put my daypack on, and turned my back on the ocean and headed upriver, the trail easy, the gradient flat.

The fish runs in the Hoh and most of the West End Olympic rivers appear to be robust, unlike many of the other West Coast runs that have been compromised due to many factors. Those West End rivers have plentiful, clean, cold water and they are without dams. The salmon, steelhead, and sea-run cutthroat can move up and down those rivers at will. The rivers are short so some steelhead are able to spawn more than once, unlike longer rivers where steelhead find the return journey too arduous. Pacific salmon, of course, die after spawning, and they litter the banks of the coastal rivers with rotting carcasses, pecked apart by gulls and bald eagles. Not only do the birds have a feast but so do the raccoons, black bears, and insects. The flesh of the salmon carries a special form of nitrogen that accumulates during their years at sea. After they spawn and die, their carcasses wash up on the banks and that marine nitrogen helps nourish the forest soils, too.

Once, I hooked a coho salmon on a coastal stream, and even before I landed the fish, the gulls flew in and gathered around me, ready for a feast. I shooed them away the best I could but they were persistent. When I finally dragged the fish toward the bank, I realized it was too far gone for the table—its silvery color long gone—so I took the fly out of its jawbone and was ready to release it, hoping it would move upstream and soon spawn. I cradled it gently for a while so it could regain its strength and avoid the birds that would otherwise try to pick it apart in the shallows. Then with a flick of its tail, the fish swam off into the deeper water and the gulls flew off as well.

Generally, the best steelheading in those rivers is during the winter and early spring, and I have spent time on the upper Quinault, Hoh, and the Queets. While the catching has always been slow, the fishing has been wonderful because of the rivers' beauty. On the Hoh I hired a guide with his drift boat one day. On the Queets and the Quinault, I have used a guide, too, using an inflatable raft in those cases. I have also fished from the bank without a guide on all those three rivers.

Most of those rivers are glacial fed with broad gravel bars, some scattered about with piles of driftwood. The violent storms from the North Pacific slam into the peninsula, the rainstorms causing the trees to shake their branches like a wet dog, the ensuing floods causing the banks to cave in and topple large spruce, cedar, and hemlock trees into the rivers. Some of those trees float downriver and end up stranded on gravel bars, their limbs ripped off, the trunks debarked and bleached with the sun.

In the winter and spring, in particular, the rivers are often roiling, the banks sliding down into the water, car-sized rootballs ripping out of the damp forest floor, boulders stuck in between gnarly, dirty roots. Sometimes those tall evergreens on the bank topple into the water and stay stuck halfway out into the river creating a boating hazard. They are called strainers, and as a boater, you want to steer clear of them. However, in the dog days of summer, those same coastal rivers are often anorexic: the current languid, nothing more than a trickle running down through the broad riverbed, the rocks dry, sun-burnt, the drift boats stored on their trailers for not even a kayak could navigate those rivers then.

A guided drift boat trip generally is the most effective way to hook winter steelhead, especially for neophyte anglers. Using a spin rod or level-wind rod, the guide puts on a plug or roe or shrimp, tosses it overboard, and places the rod into the rod holder. The client keeps his hands around a cup of coffee, the steam rising into the cold air. Then the guide using his long oars back-trolls slowly down through the run. When the rod tip twitches, the guide grabs the rod, sets the hook, and then gives it to the client who, in turn, plays the fish.

I spent years trying to learn how to fish for steelhead on my own: I found it humbling—and still do. So, I was flustered years ago when a friend of mine who had never fished told me that this steelhead fishing business seemed to be a piece of cake.

"Heck, you just sit in the boat and grab the pole when it jerks around. What's so hard about that?" my friend said. I inquired a bit more about his fishing trip: He told me about the guide and the rod holders and the thermos filled with coffee and the back-trolling and so on. I nodded my head.

For me, fishing for winter steelhead is always difficult, especially when you use fly gear. One guide I knew on the Hoh told me that if I wanted to fish with non-fly-fishing gear using bait or jigs or spoons, we might hook three to four fish a day. If we wanted to stick with fly gear only, we would be lucky to hook one fish a day. I have forsaken those winter fish from time to time because everything is against you as a fly fisherman: Because of the colder water temperatures, the fish usually lie near the bottom and are not as active as are summer steelhead, so you have to put the fly right in front of their face, which takes some doing. Plus, most winter fish scoot up the river fairly quickly compared to summer fish that spend months upon months in freshwater.

Sometimes I feel like an idiot fly-fishing for winter steelhead, day after day, cold and miserable, flaying the water, looking for the hookup that seldom arrives. You know what the definition of an idiot is? It is when you do the same thing over and over and expect to find a different result. Idiot or not, whenever I actually do hook a winter steelhead on a fly, I am particularly satisfied. I am happy too when someone else in the party hooks one; after all, it is a team effort when anglers pursue difficult prey in tough conditions.

Not too long ago I had two back-to-back winter steelhead trips on the Olympic Peninsula, or O.P. as the steelheaders say. On both trips I was accompanied by my friend Mike. On the first trip most of the rivers were too high to fish due to the rain during the past few weeks. However, the upper Quinault River was still clear and that is where we went with Michael, our guide, and his rubber raft. He told us that two days earlier a client had landed and released a twenty-pound steelhead there, a spectacular feat because a fish weighing half that amount would be considered to be a winner. It was early April and we were expecting to find only wild fish as most of the hatchery fish were gone by then.

Actually, I did not want a twenty-pounder on the end of my line. I was using a seven-weight, eleven-foot switch rod and I do not think I could ever land such a salmon-sized fish on that rod. I would have been happy with a ten-pounder, believe me.

Oddly, the sun came out for most of the day, a rarity in that country in the cold and wet months on the peninsula. As we drifted along in our raft, I noticed that the river was broad and braided, like some of the rivers in Alaska. Before too long we got out of the raft and stepped onto the rocky beach ready to do some casting. A really good Spey caster could drop the fly right in next to the far bank. I did my best using my shooting head line, heavy sink-tip, and large bright fly. My casting was not always graceful, but I was usually able to send the fly out into the main current where it would swing into the softer fishable water.

I was wading thigh deep in the cold water. The T-11 sink-tip and short ten-pound leader should have been able to deliver the fly a couple of feet from the bottom—or so I hoped. And there I hoped to connect up with a winter steelhead: It would have been in the river only a week or two earlier with its saltwater color a brilliant silver hue. The fish's mission was to swim upstream to its natal waters where the gravel would be just so, and then the fish would scoop out the gravel with its tail and create a redd. The mating and the spawning ritual would come to pass, silently and unseen except for maybe a solitary bald eagle—its talons wrapped around a hemlock branch high in the crown—its piercing yellow eyes looking down below where two long dark shapes were lithely moving about in the shallows.

Such would be my fish and I was trying to find it in the cold waters of the Quinault. I made a good cast or two and then I took a few steps downriver and cast again. The wading was not especially difficult as I shuffled along the rocky bottom; the stones were polished by the sediment-entrained water that flowed from the high mountains. The long run was about three to six feet in depth and the current was about the speed of a good walk. It was a perfect steelhead run, perfect for swinging the fly. I had enough water there for a whole day of casting, but mercifully, our guide pinpointed some of the most likely lies so I did not have to try to cover the entire run.

As the day warmed, we went floating down in our raft, down where the waters braided, where the fickle main current flowed down one channel one day and another channel the next day. We saw some downed trees at the edge of the water. Forested mountains rose up from the river's floodplain and the peaks were frosted with snow. We examined the flies and saw that most of them were colored pink or black and kingfisher blue. Some of the flies were weighted with barbell eyes or coneheads; most of them had intruder hooks that trailed out from the end of the shank, palmered with marabou feathers.

After lunch we walked down the bank and waded out as deep as possible and then began casting. Cast, mend, swing, retrieve. Over and over and over. Only a steelheader—or maybe a bonehead—would understand.

"Fish on!" Mike yelled. His Spey rod was deeply bowed and line was whirling off the spool. The green shooting head had disappeared downriver. The running line was totally gone, too. A fair amount of backing was stretched out on the water, backing that likely had not seen the light of day since it had been put on at the fly shop some time ago.

"Oh, it's a bright one," I said when I saw the fish jump. It was a good-sized steelhead, unusually deep in the body, almost more like a coho. And bright! It must have been in the river less than a week. There is nothing as brilliant as the silver sheen of a leaping steelhead on a crisp, sunny day. I know that Mike was all aboard—no multitasking, no thoughts of anything but trying to handle that strong quick fish that was trying to go back to the ocean.

When a lot of backing has spooled off the reel, you can expect trouble, even for an able steelheader like Mike. The fish ran from mid-channel into the shallower water around the outside bend where there were some short submerged willows along the edge. Somehow the line may have tangled up with that vegetation. Who knows? All we knew was that suddenly the rod was no longer bowed.

And the fish? From its point of view, the fish must have been immensely relieved that a little bunch of feathers and steel had not won out.

Damn! Big Medicine there. Watch out!

Our words were words of loss, but they evaporated quickly into the quiet blue Olympic sky. At last, Mike reeled his line back in and he and I went at it again, because where there is one fish there may well be another one—or two.

After another fifteen minutes I finally waded back toward the rocky bank—the smooth, rounded, gray stones. Maybe there were no more fish in that run. Or maybe the fish were there and simply uninterested in the gaudy kingfisher blue and black fly that was knotted onto my tippet. The big fly had been dragged down into the depths with the heavy sink-tip; the fly had been undulating and pulsating in the current near the bottom. But the fish, if there were any nearby, did not find the fly alluring and ignored my offering.

A year later Mike and I went back to the O.P. again. This time we were there in late March and the rivers were low. The upper Quinault was too low to fish and even the Queets was a bit low, but it was still fishable. On the first day we were on our own and we waded out into a couple of runs. The water conditions were good, but we did not hook any fish all the same.

The next day we hired the same guide, Michael, whom we had used the previous year. We met up early in the morning alongside a bridge, shuttled our vehicles, and lugged the raft from the trailer down into the water. The day was chilly and the sky was bright above the rumpled forested mountains, a steep terrain densely vegetated, laced with game trails, the soft moss trampled by the elk.

We took off in the raft with Michael in the middle seat as the oarsman, me in the stern, and Mike in the bow, the swirling water rushing by, its diamond chop, its pancake-like slicks. When you leave behind the ramp, you leave behind everything else: everything—no deadlines, no electronic screens. In front of you is another world you occupy for the next eight hours or so, riveted to the timeless rhythm of the river, maybe a few clouds overhead, drifting, rudderless, suspended in an otherwise empty sky, save for maybe an osprey riding the thermals, soaring, searching for fish, too.

I tucked my water bottle, extra gloves, and lunch into a waterproof bag. My limited tackle was tucked away too, just a pair of pliers, spools of leader, nipper, and a small selection of flies. The Queets and other West End rivers have wonderful swing water, perfect for casting into broad flows of moderate current and moderate depth. Some of these runs are a quarter-mile long and the intrepid winter steelheader could swing flies all day long on such water. The secret, of course, is finding where exactly in that run the fish may be. When we approached a good piece of swing water, we would beach the raft, get out, and wade out into the river. Then I would cast, let the fly sink momentarily, mend, and then swing the fly across the flow. After a few good casts, I would take four or five steps and cast out again. With steelheading you should keep moving downriver. Trout fishing is different because sometimes you might want to stay in one place for quite a while if the fish are rising in a particular back eddy or riffle. But for steelheading, especially with a fly, you need to cover a lot of water and so you should keep moving, unless, of course, you happen to know that the fish are there for sure, as when you have had a bump or a show, that telltale swirl at the end of the line. Even if you know that the fish are around, it is usually not effective to go over the same water time after time. Tie on a different fly, if you want, and sometimes that may work. But fish are not blind: They can easily see a big, bright winter fly swimming through the water. If they are not interested, well, they are not; maybe the next fish farther downriver will be interested, so wade on down the river a little farther. Of course, the best part of any run is always on the far side. Always. The angler has to wade in deep and then cast a long line to reach the fly in close to shore. Or, if the river is wide, at least get that fly out to the edge of the main current.

On a day-long float such as this, there were also long sections of the river without any decent swing water, so as we floated by the banks, we put away our Spey rods and used shorter single-handed rods. We both tied on an indicator and a jig. Michael, the oarsman, safely kept the raft going down the river through the rapids and the flatwater. At various points Mike and I each cast out our short lines upriver and across, careful not to cross each other's lines. The strike indicators floated by and the jigs were suspended some three to four feet below, allowing a fish a glimpse of the alluring bright jig as it drifted down the current. More fish are hooked on such jigs compared to swinging the fly because the jig gets right down to the bottom quickly as the current flows along; but to me, swinging the fly is more fun and more graceful, especially when the angler makes a really fine Spey cast, the line looping way out onto the water, the slick running line cutting through the winter air. And the long arc of the line as it swings across the flow is always filled with anticipation, when at any moment the line might tighten.

While there were no houses or any buildings on the banks as we floated down the river, we were not alone. We saw several drift boats floating down the river; and from time to time we saw a boat anchor-up at a promising lie, where the anglers, most likely, were using diving plugs.

Two young teenagers scooted by in their kayaks. Later I saw them beach their boats, get out, and take their spinning rods and try to catch a fish. I looked at those two boys, there on this wild river, there in their little boats, spending a fine day searching for fish, searching for fun, just searching . . . their lives pupating, as it were, beginning to emerge as adults. Oh, I am sure they were having a grand time away from home, away from school, away from homework, away from chores, and out on the river. There they were, those two boys, their youthful lives moving along with the current, just as time moves along with its own incessant current. A river and time are inexorably bound together, except that for those two boys it was a river without time for time hardly exists for a child: The past is next to nothing, the present fleeting, the future as infinite as the Olympic sky, a skyline now jagged with a sawtooth ridgeline and the ice-crusted pinnacles. Yes, a boy has all the time in the world. Black dogs are just black dogs, not the phantasmal black dogs that bedevil adults as they begin to realize that their river of time will soon shallow out. A boy wonders, from time to time, about what he will become, where he will live, what he will do, and who he will meet. But those thoughts do not last long, for he is busy casting out another silver-plated spoon, hoping that the life of the river will intercept his offering.

We waved to the boys as we passed them by, and we hoped that one day they would meet up with a strong winter steelhead. While no longer boys, we stubble-faced fishermen also hoped that a fish would intercept our terminal tackle, too, specifically a fly that I had just tied onto the tippet: a large bright pink fly with an intruder hook, hopefully so any short take by the fish would still find the hook in its mouth.

And where were the fish? Where? I did not know for I had been casting and casting all day, and the day before that, and last year on the Quinault, and before that on the Hoh: indeed, a fish of a thousand casts.

We continued floating on downriver and finally beached the raft at one especially graceful bend in the river—where the river had coursed its way up against the far side, as if a gigantic French curve template had been placed up against a long cutbank. We lumbered out of the raft, and Mike went downstream to fish and I went upstream along with Michael, our guide. He showed me a spot near the head of the run where a small eddy swirled in close to the rocky bank. The drop in that day's river level had created a slightly different hydrology than the previous day. It took me a few false casts to get my line out properly and hopefully drop the fly near the seam where the eddy and the main current met. I had the usual sink-tip on the shooting head, so I had only one attempt to throw a mend upstream before the tip and leader would vanish. I was still shuffling about trying to get a good casting platform because the bank was steep and filled with round smooth rocks that were ever ready to roll any moment downhill whenever my feet shifted about. At last I was able to make a good cast and then a small mend before the sink-tip totally disappeared. I expected that there was going to be a long arc of line slowly swinging across the run from mid-river to the shallow water. As the line began to stretch out into a broad swing, something interrupted my little plan.

"Whoa! First cast!"

The rod bowed and the line was tight in a second. The fish shot downstream, the reel humming like crazy. The fish was absolutely there, totally there, no nibble, no soft take, right on the button, the fish trying to get back to the salt as fast as possible. I had a twelve-pound tippet on the line and the drag had been cranked way down, but the fish did not seem to notice: It ran like a fish possessed. It probably had never been stung with a hook as we were less than fifteen miles from the ocean. The line was spinning off the spool and I started to run down the bank as fast as I could, but the bank was steep and rocky. I was not fleet-of-foot with my cumbersome boot-foot waders and my tethered wading staff flopping beside me. The shooting line was long gone and so was the running line. Now I was way into the backing and the spool was still singing. The backing got kinked and I tried to pry it loose. Fortunately, I was able to untangle it and the backing went spinning its way off the arbor.

The angle of repose on the talus slope was exactly where I was attempting to "run" down the riverbank, so every time I stepped gingerly, the rocks began sliding down toward the edge of the water. I scampered along the best I could to get a foothold, and all the while, the rod was danced about and line was peeling off the reel. Soon the backing became kinked again. I pulled at it and tried to unravel the #20 Dacron backing. The diameter of the backing was small, as is most backing, so picking at the kinks in that thin line with my cold thick fingers was daunting. For the life of me, I could not undo that tightly wound snarl in the backing.

Who in the hell put that backing on anyway?

(Probably me.)

"The backing's stuck," I said to Michael, who was nearby. He looked over at the reel. Not good. He asked me if I wanted him to take the rod and run with it. He was younger than me, more agile, and would be better able to run faster with the rod downriver than I could.

"Take it!"

I gave Michael the rod and he began running down the bank with it, the rockfall clatter loud and clear. Despite the stout tippet, I was afraid it might break because of the nasty snarl in the backing and because the fish seemed determined to go back to the ocean. I continued stumbling along down the steep bank.

Eventually, the fish paused, the bank leveled out a bit, and I was able to meet up with Michael and he handed the rod back to me. By then we had a great deal of line in the air so the line was not nearly as taut as it should be. Barbless hooks are required in those waters, and more than often when you are fast to a fish with a barbless hook in its mouth, it can easily shake the hook if there is any slack in the line at all. Michael grabbed onto the line and kept it taut, keeping the line from swinging about in the air. I pumped the rod upwards. Then I slowly dropped the rod back down and I was able to reel in a few inches of line. Then I pumped the rod back upwards again. Over and over it went. Together we slowly walked down the beach toward where the fish was thrashing about in the middle of the river, not wanting to run any farther, but not wanting to surrender either.

Eventually, I got most of the backing onto the spool. By then Michael had released his grip on the line and it was taut all the way from the fish to me. After I was able to reel in about half of the running line, the fish seemed to see me and it bolted, but not too far. I was able to regain the line back in another five minutes and continued to reel in more line. Michael hustled over to the raft, grabbed the net, and walked back to me where the fish was beginning to tire.

Below the cobbled beach was the bluish-turquoise water and within it was a silvery fish, absolutely fresh and bright, moving around in the shallows, likely unhappy about where it was, wishing that, instead, it was far downriver, back in more familiar waters where there was a bit of brine to it. The adipose fin was intact, and we were going to release the fish as gently as possible. The fish had done all it could do: With an estimated weight of ten pounds, its fight was valiant, but it was overwhelmed by a two-hundred-pound humanoid, whom while short on native instinct was long on intelligence, an intelligence that the fish could not imagine.

As it was, the fish was my captive at the moment as it laid in the net resting in the shallows while I tried to take the hook out of its jaw-bone. The hook came out easily. The fish was especially heavily bodied and I grasped the wrist of its slick and muscular body and looked up at Michael while he snapped a picture of me and the fish. He took a few steps over toward me and showed the picture on his phone/camera. He did a good job. He made the fish look like what, in fact, it was and not like a whale. Way too many big fish pictures in various angling mag-azines *appear* to be huge, simply because the angler extends his arms and reaches out his fish toward the photographer, putting the fish in the foreground and the angler in the background. A silly trick, it seems to me. *My* fish was big and beautiful just as it was. No need to gild the lily, as Shakespeare would say.

(Later at the end of the day, I sent off that picture electronically to several people—shameless braggart that I am—along with a short text: "On the Queets. On the swing.")

With the photo-op over, I slid the fish out of the net and continued to hold it gently. When the time was ready, it would swim away and its captivity would be over. It would swim back into the dark waters. Later it would swim upriver to find its spawning waters, maybe a little feeder stream, the riverbed gravel ready to be upended.

And yes . . . after a few more minutes . . . it came to pass . . . and the fish slapped its tail and then it disappeared into the current.

The rest of the day was a blur to me. Mike connected later with a nice fish. We floated on down the river, bend upon bend, to where a painted rock on the bank marked the boundary of the Queets Indian Reservation, where we, as non–tribal members, were no longer allowed to fish any farther downriver. We pulled in our lines, and a hundred yards farther down, we saw the dirt ramp under the bridge.

We beached the raft, walked up to my car, and Michael and I drove together back upriver to where Michael had parked his pickup and trailer early in the morning. He got into his pickup and then we each drove our own vehicles back to the moored raft, put it on the trailer, and said our farewells.

As we drove down the highway over the divide between the Queets and the Quinault, the clouds began to darken and I searched for the right words to sum up the day. Suddenly, I thought of a little barn spider named Charlotte who once spun two words into its web saying, "Some Pig."

My word search was over: "Some Fish."

CHAPTER NINE

The Leaper

THE MOUNTAINS OF THE OLYMPIC PENINSULA ARE SPECTACULAR, indeed, whether they are viewed today from Seattle or out at sea where a Spanish navigator named Juan Perez first sighted them in 1774. Fourteen years later a British captain named John Meares also was enamored by the Olympic Mountains and he named the biggest peak Mount Olympus. Many of the geographical names nearby were later ascribed to local tribes, such as the Hoh, Quinault, Queets, Quileute, Makah, and the Ozette. However, it is curious that some of the Pacific Northwest's most prominent features were named after people who had never seen them. One of the first Northwest name droppers was, of course, British captain George Vancouver during his exploration in the 1790s. While charting Puget Sound, Captain Vancouver sighted a large, snow-clad mountain and named it after one of his naval superiors, Rear Admiral Peter Rainier. Later during the same year in 1792, his expedition traveled up the Columbia River, and they named a large mountain to the east and south of the river for another British admiral named Lord Samuel Hood. Neither Admiral Hood nor Admiral Rainier had ever laid eyes on the North Pacific or the Northwest's two most iconic mountains. Moreover, both Royal Navy officers had fought against the American Revolution a decade earlier. Admiral Hood was one of the two main British naval commanders at the decisive Battle of the Capes in 1781 where the French fleet outmaneuvered the British and enabled the Americans to defeat the British at Yorktown.

But back to the Olympic Peninsula: Its largest rivers, such as the Queets and the Hoh, are on the west side of the peninsula due to the immense amount of rain clouds that sweep in from the North Pacific. The water-laden clouds rise up in elevation as they bump into the mountains and drop their load, be it rain or snow. After those clouds get over the crest, they are much lighter, precipitate much less, and essentially create a rain shadow for much of the eastern side of the peninsula and even some of the Puget Sound islands. Not surprisingly, the rivers that flow east of the Olympics' crest are fewer in number and in volume.

The largest river that flows from the east side of the peninsula is the Skokomish River. Still, it is a decent-sized river and when it floods it spills over its banks, the water spreading across the roads and into the dairy pastures. Sometimes the migrating salmon have trouble finding the river's channel during high-water times, and the fish swim into the flooded pastures where they can get stranded when the waters recede. I have an old newspaper photograph that shows a chum salmon literally crawling across a rural highway where the Skokomish jumped its banks and flooded the road and pasturelands. In the photograph you can see the ditch on the far side of the road where the chum were finning about in foot-deep water, getting ready to scoot across the road and get back down to the river.

The salmon somehow knew in their own instinctive way that if the water level in the ditch continued to drop that they would perish. They had to get to the other side. In the photograph one of the more adventurous fish wiggled its way out of the ditch and onto the flooded, slickened road. The fish apparently used its strong tail and wiggled back and forth crawling across the pavement on its belly, but by the time it got across to the yellow centerline, or the crown of the road, the water had thinned out to less than an inch deep. That is where the photographer snapped the shot. Hopefully, the fish wiggled one more time, maybe two more times, and got across the road to the other side. Or maybe a Good Samaritan got out of the car and pushed the fish off the road into the deeper water. The perseverance of salmon bound for their spawning waters is beyond measure: They are able to swim great distances, some of them swimming upriver nearly a thousand miles from the ocean up into the Idaho mountains at five thousand feet just to find the right natal waters.

Along the coastal rivers the salmon and steelhead have much shorter distances to go to their spawning waters than do the fish bound to Idaho and the upper Columbia. I have been to a number of coastal rivers where chum salmon, in particular, begin their spawning ritual at the first gravel bar above tidewater. I used to fish for those chum on some of the Oregon north coast rivers such as the Miami and Klichis where the fish were thick in those small rivers, the fish thrashing about in the shallows, the females ready to work on their redds—all less than five miles from saltwater. Many of those salmon already had turned color in the bay and no longer had a bright silver color sheen to them, but instead had a yellowish, green tinge to them with black vertical stripes on their flanks. We anglers avoided those spawning gravel bars and sought out the deeper, swifter water where the fresher chums were migrating farther upriver. Those fresh fish, up to twelve pounds or so, can be great fighters—and if they are really fresh, they can still be good eating. Moreover, in my experience a fresh chum will take a fly more willingly in freshwater than do most any other Pacific salmon subspecies: pink, sockeye, coho, or Chinook. Some coho will want to chase a fly in freshwater, too, but I have been disappointed in the remaining three subspecies whenever I have fly-fished for them in freshwater. Yes, I have hooked those fish with a fly, but it seemed that it was only because the fly drifted its way into the fish's mouth and not because the fish willingly snapped at the fly. Others may disagree, but such is my experience with fly fishing for salmon in freshwater. More field research needed, of course.

To the south of the Olympics are two large bays along the Washington coast: Grays Harbor and Willapa Bay. A number of rivers flow into those bays. In fact, Willapa Bay is the second-largest estuary in the Lower 48 on the West Coast; only the San Francisco Bay is larger. Interestingly, the human populations of those two largest Pacific bays differ greatly: The San Francisco Bay area has a population of about seven million people, while the Willapa Bay area has a population of about twenty thousand. Many of the rivers flowing into the two Washington bays are smaller rivers with good fisheries, much like many of the other coastal rivers in Oregon and down into northern California.

One of the distinctive characteristics on the West Coast is that the distance from the beach to the mountains is but a few miles, unlike the Gulf Coast and much of the Atlantic's East Coast. The reach of tide for most coastal rivers is only a few miles, with the banks on each side dotted with pastures and dairy farms. Then the terrain begins to steepen and soon the once flatwater rivers become studded with rapids. The coastal angler might be able to utilize a motorized boat a few miles beyond tidewater, but at a certain point the shallow bars and rapids will preclude motorboats and the drift boats will be his best watercraft. Still farther upriver, the rapids will become too intense and only the inflatable boats will be of use. Farther upstream still, even that will not work and it will be a walk-and-wade operation. The entire navigable distance of a rainforest river from beach to walk-and-wade fishing can be less than twenty miles.

While I have experienced some robust Olympic Peninsula rivers and their strong winter steelhead, nonetheless I have caught more fish farther south on some of the smaller rainforest coastal rivers, often the type that are too small to navigate with a drift boat. On a small coastal river, you have to walk and wade or perhaps use a small pram or one-man inflatable raft. The small coastal rivers are especially enticing because the fish can be large even though the waters are small. Such rivers have an intimacy that larger rivers lack. Normally, small intimate streams are for smaller fish, such as trout. So, it is a treat to find a large fish, such as a salmon or steelhead, in small water.

By nature smaller rivers cannot withstand much angling pressure, so I will not reveal the real name of one of my favorite little coastal rivers; instead I will call it the Crown River.

Not long ago I hiked down to the Crown River and attempted to cross it. The water was clear and near midstream the flow was swift; I waded into the river knee deep and put my wading staff down into the gravel, step by step. It was a mild and cloudy late-February day, but it was February, after all, and I did not want to fall in and get wet. I noticed under the surface of the water the aggregate bottom was barely stable, the sparkling, marble-sized gravel creeping along, bedload on the move.

A few miles downstream, tidewater would arrive in its own slow rhythmic way and the suspended load would no longer be the fine gravel that was under my feet now. As the river slowed with the tidal influence, the suspended load would be of silt. A river's sediment, like sugar in a cup of tea, courses its way out into a delta, a wetland, a floodplain, a place to drop its load, for even a small river has a heavy burden. Hydrologists say that the Mississippi River delivers more than one hundred million tons a year of sediment flowing out into the Gulf of Mexico. The small coastal rivers obviously measure their sediment load in less than millions of tons, but all the same a lot of sediment drops out into the mouth of any river. At some places where these smaller rivers flow directly into the ocean, a bar often forms, and salmon are unable to get over those bars. When a storm brews and the clouds commence to rain, the locals know when to call in sick for work because they know that the rain will raise the level of the river and the stronger current will blow out the bar. The fish, which had been kegged up for weeks, are suddenly able to swim up the river into the arms of the waiting anglers.

The current that flowed around my wadered legs had a good clip to it, the thin water clattering over the rocks. The footing was easy on the gravel and I had no problem getting to the far side. I hoisted myself up the bank by grabbing onto an exposed root.

The day before, Frank and I had each hooked a steelhead, that time using fly rod gear. On some days while fishing on coastal rivers, I use a fly rod with a sink-tip, short leader, and various flies, mostly brightly colored and large. On other days, depending on the river level, I use a level-wind reel and rod with a float and a jig, some black, others green, and several with pink and flame red. On this particular day I was using my level-wind outfit because the run I had planned to fish was difficult to fish with a fly.

I first walked over to a likely spot on the river and cast out up against a steep bank where the water was dark and probably five feet deep. I watched the float as it drifted down and mended the line so the float would not drag. I wanted the small pink jig to be suspended about a foot above the bottom. The visibility was about three to four feet deep. I had to be careful because of the overhanging trees. Bereft of leaves the branches had a way of reaching out and grabbing tackle: Every now and then I would find a bright-colored jig or lure or fly hanging high in a tree, an angling Christmas tree.

A little later I hiked farther down the trail, edging along the bank, the light slowly leaving for another day. Actually, the winter light is seldom bright along the North Pacific coast as the sun is low on the horizon in these latitudes during that time. And more than often the clouds are always hovering about. I was within a few miles of saltwater, and the air had a tang to it and also a fecund moisture of the nearby tidal flats dewatered by the ebb tide. Out beyond toward the west, where the river flowed into the sea, was the Pacific Ocean, a very different piece of water than was the small river where I was fishing. The ocean: too big, like the firmament of the midnight sky, too big. At times it appears to be benevolent, the rounded swells, smooth and rolling.

But the ocean has many faces, as Herman Melville best said in his novel *Moby-Dick*: "these are times of dreamy quietude, when beholding the tranquil beauty and brilliancy of the ocean's skin, one forgets the tiger heart that pants beneath it; and would not willing remember, that this velvet paw but conceals a remorseless fang."

Crown River is but a spit in the ocean, but that is where I was on that day. After hiking another twenty yards farther, I climbed down a cutbank to a little spot where I could stand right next to the water. I slid the float down on the line about three and a half feet from the jig and put a small split-shot on the leader about halfway in between. I first cast it out upstream. The float drifted by. Below it was the jig, its wispy marabou feathers waving back and forth in the current a foot or so above the rocky bottom. I cast again and again.

I looked out at the country on either side of the river, and while there were a few newer homes back away from the banks, on the whole the area had seen better days, a century ago when the salmon canneries and lumber mills were booming. Most of the West Coast from the Olympic Peninsula down to northern California has been heavily logged since the late 1800s. Douglas fir trees as large as three hundred feet tall and ten feet in diameter were felled decade after decade. As an elderly neighbor of mine once told me about the decline of the West Coast logging industry:

"There's no logs any more nowadays, just poles." And the salmon fishing, too, is nothing compared to the days of old. Some fifty Columbia River canneries shipped as much as thirty million one-pound cans of salmon annually in the mid-1880s.

Today most tidewater rivers are studded with derelict pilings that once supported those fish-processing plants. And many lumber mill towns up and down the coast are no longer operating either: skeleton plants, abandoned, rotted with mildew, the steel rusted. Many of those sad-eyed mill towns are virtually empty, places where boys and girls once marched off to school, places where men and women once felled and milled the tall Douglas fir trees manufacturing lumber and plywood. A few of those houses are still standing: rickety and dilapidated, blackberry vines reaching in between the broken panes of the bedroom windows, a carpet of moss on the roof slowly collapsing with the incessant pounding of the coastal rain. Some of the mill towns were simply razed once the timber was gone, such as Valsetz in Oregon's Coast Range. People were born there, grew up there, and moved away. Later they came back to see the old homestead and instead of a town there was nothing, slicked off like an eviscerated mudslide.

There are many places in the wild areas of the West that may be called empty—from rugged forested mountains to deserts. But there are places that are less than empty, places where people once lived and loved, where there now is no longer the sound of a human voice, where the salal and vine maple and alder of the thickly vegetated coastal mountains have rooted their way into a land that was once peopled and no longer is. A depopulated place such as that is less than empty: It is a *despoblado* place, as the Mexicans would say.

Looking back at the river, I kept casting the jig out again and again. Then I slid the float up the line to four feet above the jig as there was a channel of bedrock that appeared to be a bit deeper than I had first anticipated, what the river runners call a thalweg, the deepest thread in a river's current. I took off the pink-colored jig and replaced it with a jig that had a mix of orange and white feather fibers along with some Krystal Flash strands trailing off the hook. I cast the jig out. The float drifted down the current, lifeless, somnolent it seemed, but ready at any moment to spring back to life. I cast it out again.

Suddenly, the float disappeared into a menacing, sucking boil of water. Out of it rocketed a silver-bright steelhead, fresh from the salt. There was no rainbow color to its flanks; it was all silver. As silver as it was, it looked more like a coho salmon, except that steelhead are slimmer than coho. It was, indeed, a steelhead and I could see it easily because it ran straight toward me and then jumped high in the air. There was no tail-walking as some steelhead do; instead the large fish went horizontal in the air a good foot above the water's surface. I was dumbfounded. I gathered my wits and realized that there was slack line all over the water because the fish had run toward me. I tried to reel in the line as fast as I could, but before I could the fish jumped high in the air again and crashed down onto the water's surface with a resounding slap. The fish and I were not more than twenty feet apart and there was still slack line on the water. I reeled in some more line and again the fish jumped, this time its head tossing back and forth in the air.

The fish did not seem to like the sting of the jig. Maybe earlier in the day, it had been schooled-up in tidewater, its gills beginning to adapt to freshwater. A day or two before that, it likely was swimming in the ocean, chasing after shrimp or maybe squid. Somehow it knew that it was time to move on, the spawning impulse was upon it. Somehow it knew what river to run up and how far. Some people claim these anadromous fish have a memory bank going back to when they were young, back when they were eating mayfly nymphs as youngsters, readying to grow into smolts and get downriver to the ocean. These fish may have a magnetic sense of where their natal waters are and how to get there. Plus, maybe they have an acute sense of smell and can distinguish the chemistry of a particular river that they want to ascend. Whatever it is, the steelhead, my steelhead, had schooled-up in the bay and finally found the right time to swim out of the saltwater and into the right river and, miraculously, onto the end of my line.

Again the fish jumped, four times in less than two minutes. Or maybe it was one minute. Or maybe it was five minutes. I could not tell you because time was on vacation. I was in the zone and everything else had faded away but the fish and me. The rod was throbbing, spastic, cold river water flowing by me, water coming down from the hills, rushing down from the mountains, plunging down through the canyons, over waterfalls and cascades, cold waters melted from snowbanks, down into the foothills and out onto the floodplain. The river was the medium of the spawn, life under the gravel, eggs bursting their round little forms, animate and alive. From alevins to smolts they were flushed down the river, pastured in the ocean, and later returned to the river. And there they were, returning to their nursery waters after years from their wanderings in the ocean, weighing anywhere from four pounds to fifteen pounds. So when a large fish is attached to your line, nothing else exists: Time is suspended and all other thoughts in your consciousness have vanished; you are in the moment.

And the fish? For some unfathomable reason the fish opened its mouth to bite down on an undulating bright assemblage of feathers and steel. The fish likely tried to spit out the jig, but it was too late. Then it did what it instinctively tried to do—to try to get that damn sharp object out of its mouth. It was full of ocean life, strong and sleek.

And then . . . then . . . all of a sudden it was off the hook: The wet marabou feathers and the sharp steel were no longer in the fish's mouth. The fish swam off to sulk, maybe to hunker down under a bedrock ledge, deeply shadowed where no predators could find it.

And where did the time go when all this happened? Like a game of basketball, it was time out. The drumbeat of Father Time had disappeared, suspended for a graceful moment. The fish had been leaping and running all over the river, and my unblinking eyes had been riveted on the line where it had cut through the water like a knife, carving through the opaque liquid around me. Then at that moment there was no yesterday, no tomorrow, just existence—transient and eternal at once.

The light had weakened by now, the backdrop of naked alders and immense cedar trees was darkening, and all the while the river kept flowing by, relentlessly, effortlessly, for a river never sleeps. I thought of the fight just minutes before and how usually a fish runs away from the angler and the line is then fast to the fish. This time it was just the opposite. With a slack line a fish can jump, wag its head back and forth, and cause the hook to fall out of its mouth. And after the fourth jump that apparently is what happened, because by the time I finally reeled in the line, there was nothing on the end of it except the float and the jig.

Disappointed?

I cannot tell you how deep was the hollow feeling that I had—from ecstasy to less than empty. I sat down on the bank and rested. I took a swig from my small water bottle and then wearily trudged back down the trail, the sky overcast as ever, the stratus clouds right down on the deck, the sunset masked. I walked back across the same ford and then went slipping and sliding up the muddy bank, the ferns and blackberry bushes poking at me. I carefully put my wading staff down into the soft earth and hoisted myself up over the lip of the bank. I hiked along the trail through a tangle of vegetation and by then darkness was upon me, thickening as only the dark can, ready to compress my world around me, the very air suddenly close as I gingerly hiked through the moonless wood.

Later, after I took off my waders and had a cold beer before me, I told my friend Frank about the fish, its jump upon jump. We talked awhile about how steelhead and salmon are close cousins, and that the word salmon stems from the Latin word *salmo*, which roughly translates as leaping fish. So, we called the fish The Leaper.

Where The Leaper went we will never know. I do not know whether it was a hen or a buck. Generally, I think that female steelhead jump more often than do the bucks, but some anglers think that is nonsense. My only thought was that I hoped that The Leaper had continued upriver after its battle with me and eventually spread its spawn—milt or eggs, whatever it was—onto the waters, its nascent life sinking down into the river, nestled down into the gravel. And in the years ahead, hopefully those genes would continue on, its progeny fit and strong, ready for the next journey from the river to the sea and back again: gravel to gravel, as they say.

Section III
Northern California Rivers

CHAPTER TEN

The Klamath and Ol' Iron-Ass VP

WHILE THE KLAMATH RIVER FLOWS DIRECTLY INTO THE PACIFIC Ocean, it is not considered a coastal river per se because it does not rise out of coastal mountains. Instead, the Klamath begins far to the east; in fact, the Klamath is the only river other than the Columbia and the Pit River that have their headwaters east of the Cascades and flow all the way to the Pacific. Straddling the California-Oregon border, the Klamath is a tortuous river, both geographically and politically. While its watershed is thinly populated, it miraculously has been the center of attention not only in the West but twenty-seven hundred miles away in Washington, DC. The environmental controversy over the Klamath's water and fish includes dozens of players, including county commissioners, governors, Indian tribes, farmers, environmentalists, fishermen, lawyers, federal bureaucrats, and even a top federal elected official who in the early years of the new millennium allegedly masterminded a farmer-friendly water policy on the Klamath River that later resulted in the largest salmon kill in the United States.

But first, the Klamath's tortured geography must be appreciated before you can understand its tortured politics. The Klamath River is an upside-down river. The headwaters of most western rivers are in steep mountains, and many of them are glaciated. Those areas usually have few if any towns nearby. As most rivers flow downstream, the towns grow in size, the terrain flattens out, and the landscape changes from forest to agriculture.

The headwaters of the 260-mile-long Klamath River begin in a high-elevation plateau, just to the east of the Cascade Range. Upon that plateau is one of the West's largest lakes, Upper Klamath Lake, measuring some twenty miles long and eight miles wide. Three headwater rivers flow into the lake, and the outlet of the lake is the beginning of the Klamath River. Thanks to a large federal irrigation project, the plateau reaps an agricultural bounty, from potatoes to horseradish to beef cattle that graze on thousands of acres of pasture land. The land is well tended with hundreds of farms that surround the region's largest city, Klamath Falls, with a population of twenty-two thousand people.

Shortly after the river flows out of the lake, it digs down into a rugged canyon and courses its way into the Cascade Mountains and the Klamath Mountains. The river cuts away through the wrinkled Earth's crust mile upon mile all the way to the ocean. While the river churns along down in the canyon, the thinly forested dry country on top is lean; its agricultural production is lean, too, save for a few beef cattle. The area's major town in the midsection of the river is called Yreka, with a population of fewer than eight thousand. Tributaries flow into the Klamath from the Shasta, Scott, and Trinity Rivers, and by the time the river empties into the Pacific Ocean, the human population includes only a few homes near the unincorporated hamlet of Requa, a once-booming salmon cannery and logging town. There the river gushes out of a portal through the redwood forests and into the ocean without much of a broad floodplain or delta. At its terminus it finally snakes its way biting through the shifting sand bars and finally churns its way into the Big Salt. At times the flood tide and river's current clash and create a froth of whitecaps along the deserted beach—the thirty-nine million Californians somewhere else—the spindrift dancing across the wet sand soon to perish in the salty air, the river totally spent, its waters dissipated, absorbed into that which it cannot measure nor comprehend.

The northern California coast along the Klamath is shrouded with fog, where the tallest trees in the world take their moisture out of the air, when they were alive back in the days of kings and queens and castles and crusades. The redwoods are a land where tall men no longer feel tall, where everyone feels as though they are dwarfs, where the tree trunks rise upwards seemingly forever into the mist.

While accustomed to big trees from the Olympics to Oregon's rain-forest, I have had to take my hat off to the redwoods whenever I have traveled there. Once we stayed overnight at the Requa Inn at the mouth of the Klamath River. Across the US Highway 101 bridge and down the road was the Redwoods National Park. There on a trail hiking through those giants, there was a splendid grove of redwoods, and on that marker were some words written by former first lady Lady Bird Johnson, wife of President Lyndon Johnson. By the mid-1960s the old-growth redwoods were about to be gone, and it was Lady Bird who helped keep the chain-saws at bay and helped establish the area as a national park.

One of my most unforgettable memories of the past years is walking through the redwoods last November seeing the lovely shafts of light filtering through the trees so far above, feeling the majesty and silence of that forest, and watching a salmon rise in one of those swift streams—all our problems seemed to fall into perspective and I think every one of us walked out more serene and happier.

—Lady Bird Johnson
July 30, 1969
Redwoods National Park

I could not have said it better, so I scribbled down her words in my notebook. It was a muted day, a sieve of branches filtering through the sunlight. There were little hollows in the burned-out redwood trunks big enough for a couple to hunker down in a squall. The air was cool, a mix of salt and conifer, the ground sodden, tan colored, the rust-red bark thick as armor, impervious to the elements. Unlike Lady Bird, I did not see a salmon in the stream where we hiked along the trail, but then again she was there in the fall and my wife and I were there in the summer. Most likely the salmon that Lady Bird witnessed were fall Chinook, the most plentiful salmon around there.

Even today after the destruction of the salmon runs along California's north coast, those indomitable fish soldier on. The Klamath once was the third-largest producer of salmon in the Lower 48, after the

Columbia and the Sacramento Rivers. At Requa back in the 1920s, cannery workers processed as much as ten thousand salmon a day. Even today, despite the water diversions, habitat destruction, and dams, more than one hundred thousand fall Chinook enter the Klamath River annually, though the runs vary greatly over the years. Much of the Klamath salmon's migration was blocked after a series of dams were built in the upper river in the early 1900s. Above those dams, however, are resident rainbow trout that grow to an outrageous size due to the nutrient-rich Upper Klamath Lake. I have tried to catch those monsters . . . but . . . I am ahead of myself.

For the moment I want you to better understand about the Klamath River's strange geography: It is, indeed, an upside-down river because its headwaters are flat and populated by towns and farms, and the farther down the river goes, the more rugged it becomes with fewer and fewer towns along the way. Moreover, most of the water in the Klamath's largest tributary, the Trinity River, actually flows into another watershed, thereby depriving the Klamath's flow and its fish runs. The 165-mile Trinity begins its way through the Scott Mountains from north to south, and then it turns back north and finally flows into the Klamath River. The Trinity once had a robust salmon run, but it never had a fertile valley and a large population. Along its serpentine route from the mountains to the confluence of the Klamath, the Trinity flows within a few miles of the Sacramento River, just downstream of Shasta Dam. After the dam was completed in World War II, the resulting massive reservoir created seemingly ample water for the almond orchards, olive groves, and rice paddies in the Sacramento Valley. But it seems that there is never enough when it comes to California's water needs. A few years later farmers, politicians, hydrologists, and civil engineers took a hard look at the Trinity—its water just flowed out into the ocean, unused and underutilized.

Before too long the planners went to work to find a way to get that Trinity "surplus" water across the divide and into the Sacramento watershed. By the early 1960s there were two dams on the Trinity and an eleven-mile-long tunnel large enough to drive a car through. Since then, most of the upper Trinity's water has flowed through that tunnel, through the Trinity mountains and into a reservoir. In turn, that same water in the reservoir goes through another, shorter tunnel and eventually down into the Sacramento. As a result, some one hundred miles of spawning waters on the upper Trinity was blocked off, the water volume of the Trinity below the dams has been sharply reduced, the habitat has been altered, and the once plentiful Trinity salmon runs are a thing of the past.

While most of the Trinity's water has been diverted into a different watershed, so the Klamath's water has been diverted in yet another way. The huge ninety-six-square-mile Upper Klamath Lake, the headwaters of the Klamath River, appears to have more than enough water, but it is a shallow lake and rainfall is low in the high-elevation plateau, an estimated fourteen inches annually. When rain and snow is adequate, all is well, but when the rain clouds no longer arrive and the snowpack is lean, then there can be trouble. Prior to European settlement this arrangement worked out well, but in 1905 the US Bureau of Reclamation, under the Department of Interior, launched one of the country's earliest federal irrigation projects in the two-state area of the Klamath basin. Once there was a Lower and Upper Klamath Lake, but the lower one was soon drained and made into cropland. Over time, more and more of the water in Upper Klamath Lake was diverted to agricultural use, too.

In 2001, after a severe drought, federal regulators reduced the irrigation allotment to maintain a minimal amount of water in the Klamath River and Upper Klamath Lake for fish survival. Low water levels and warm water can cause diseases for cold-water fish, such as salmon, trout, and steelhead. At the time, the Klamath coho salmon and two species of suckers were listed under the federal Endangered Species Act. Tribal, commercial, and sport fishermen and conservationists urged the National Marine Fisheries Service, under the Department of Commerce, to keep the water flowing down the river so salmon could migrate and spawn. On the other hand, farmers urged the bureau to divert the river's flow through irrigation canals and onto their thirsty croplands.

Protests erupted and some overly zealous people illegally reopened the irrigation headgates that had been closed and let the water flow into the canals. Later federal marshals shut the gates again. Top Department of Interior officials did their best to assuage the angry irrigators on the 225,000-acre project, but the conflict over water and fish was nasty and the noise was heard thousands of miles away, all the way to the banks of another river, the Potomac.

One of the federal officials who heard the Klamath ruckus was Dick Cheney, then vice president under President George W. Bush. While a deft Washington insider, Cheney was all the same a Westerner for he represented Wyoming when he was in Congress. His lengthy resume included White House chief of staff under President Gerald Ford and secretary of defense under President George H. W. Bush. During all these years he regularly traveled back to his western haunts for his R & R. The din of the Klamath controversy troubled him: Croplands and pastures—an entire rural economy—were drying up because of a few fish. Two major federal departments—Department of Commerce and Department of Interior—were at cross purposes: one trying to keep water in the river and the other one trying to siphon it out. And in the middle was a Republican administration that had as its constituency a rural, western, pro-Republican populace.

At the time, I was a Northwest news correspondent covering the environment, and I wrote a number of stories about the Klamath controversy. Myself and other journalists speculated that Cheney and Karl Rove, political advisor and deputy chief of staff under Bush, may have had more than just a passing interest in the faraway, sparsely settled Klamath basin, but there was little evidence of such direct involvement. Only much later did I learn that Cheney allegedly had pressured the Department of Interior in fashioning a new Klamath water policy that benefited farmers.

It was six years later, in fact, on June 27, 2007, when a pair of *Washington Post* reporters published a story about Cheney's involvement in the Klamath controversy. The headline was "Leaving No Tracks." According to the *Post*'s story, Cheney was on point right at the beginning of the Klamath controversy. He realized that a frontal assault on the Endangered Species Act fish listings would be difficult, plus that was not his modus operandi. Instead, he allegedly leaned on federal bureaucrats who, in turn, strongly suggested that the scientists might want to revise their studies on the threatened fish. Those revised studies showed that diverting the Klamath's water would not necessarily harm the listed fish. Many others said that those revised studies were a bit of a stretch, but all the same, by early in 2002 the bureau switched to a new ten-year plan for water flows in the upper Klamath basin. That plan called for lower minimum Klamath River flows than in the previous plan. Not surprisingly, there were no Cheney fingerprints on the new plan.

In the 2002 irrigation season, the water flowed freely out onto the croplands, despite the ongoing drought conditions. By the summer the usual salmon migration had a tough time because the water level in the river was low and getting lower. By late August and September, many of the coho and fall Chinook were diseased, and they were slowly suffocating. Low warm water and overcrowding helped created an environment where a deadly parasite was able to spread among the fish. The parasite caused the fish's once bright, blood-rich gills to turn brown and rot; in short, the fish's "lungs" no longer were able to extract liquid oxygen out of the water. By the end of September, more than thirty-three thousand fish were dead on the banks of the lower reaches of the river, the largest salmon kill in US history. The stench of the bloated fish piled up along the banks was overpowering—but the bald eagles, gulls, and black bears had a feast.

And Cheney?

Apparently, the record is silent. Stolid as ever with his lopsided smile, most of us will never know about him as a person, about his thoughts on the Klamath or many other things. Some people, such as Cheney's former boss, President George H. W. Bush, did know something about Cheney, the man. In his later years Cheney was: "Just iron-ass . . . he just became very hard-line and very different from the Dick Cheney I knew and worked with," Bush told Jon Meacham, the author of *Destiny and Power: The American Odyssey of George Herbert Walker Bush*, published in 2015.

I have always wondered about Cheney and the Klamath, because reportedly he is an avid fly fisherman, and most fly anglers want to protect and enhance the fish and their habitat. I have been told that Cheney is a proficient fly angler, a good caster, and likes to regularly fish the south fork of the Snake River in southeast Idaho. I have read stories about his fishing trips and apparently he is an amiable boat mate on the water, generous to the guides and respectful to the fish and its surroundings. And yet . . .

Meanwhile, after the 2002 fish kill, the federal agencies, Indian tribes, farmers, various state and local governmental officials, fishermen, and others got tangled up in court for years. In 2010 a much-anticipated Klamath agreement over fish and water allocations was ironed out between the various parties, but Congress failed to sign the agreement in 2015. The conflict over resolving the water diversions may go on for some time. However, in a related issue, Klamath salmon restoration efforts may find a big boost if the four hydroelectric dams along the Oregon-California border are removed. A proposal seeking to remove the dams is currently before government regulators, but as usual, a number of parties will have to sign off on the deal. If they do so, it would be one of the largest dam removals in the country.

———

Fish politics can drive you crazy and sometimes it is best to unplug and just go fishing. And that is what I have done for the last few years to try to catch one of those monster Klamath Lake trout, what the locals call "two-footers." My Klamath fishing experience has been in the headwaters, the rivers that flow into the lake and the lake itself; and I have caught trout in those rivers—but not yet a two-footer. The Klamath headwaters are a lonely and splendid country, midway between Portland and San Francisco. At forty-one hundred feet, the country is just south and east of Crater Lake, a transition zone between the Cascade Range and the Basin and Range province of the northern Great Basin. The Klamath Indians have been living there for thousands of years around the marshes, a migratory resting spot for millions of ducks, geese, and other birds. The Klamath Indians still have a reservation in the headwaters area. Downriver at the mouth of the Trinity River is the Hoopa Reservation, and at the mouth of the Klamath itself is the Yurok Reservation. The first white explorers in the Klamath basin were from the Hudson's Bay Company seeking furs in the 1820s. After the California Gold Rush of 1849 came the miners. Later came the cattle barons, then the loggers, and then the farmers of today.

When I first came into this country, I was not enthusiastic about it because of its flat terrain and extensive marshes. Like many Westerners, I like vertical terrain: mountains, canyons, talus slopes, sawtooth ridges, and ocean headlands. In contrast, the Klamath basin is more horizontal; it is a high-elevation plateau, treed with ponderosa pines, sugar pines, Douglas fir, oak, and madrone surrounding the vast marshes and laser-leveled plowed fields. The hills to the east are thinly forested and, beyond that, sagebrush country all the way to the Rockies. To the west, the Cascades rise above the flat land, but they have a rolling feel to them, less jagged than to the north. The temperatures vary from near zero in the winter to over 100 degrees Fahrenheit in the summer. The Upper Klamath Lake is the upper end of the Klamath basin. It is a huge body of water as anyone knows who has driven along US Highway 97, but on the whole it is not an especially scenic lake compared to many nearby mountain lakes, such as Crater Lake, which is a national park and where almost a half a million people visit annually.

By contrast, Upper Klamath Lake is one of the shallowest large lakes in the West with an average depth of fourteen feet. It has nearly five times the surface area of Crater Lake, its shoreline is rimmed by reeds and marshes, and it has a few beaches for swimming and other water sports. The color of the water in the lake is more green than blue, and while that may be disappointing to some, it is just fine for anglers because there are more fish in a shallow, nutrient-rich lake than there are in a deep lake with steep shorelines. And fish do love Upper Klamath Lake. Rainbow trout grow quickly and large in that inland sea. The aquatic vegetation in the shallow lake nurtures a cornucopia of life from zooplankton to aquatic insects to leeches to minnows, trout, pelicans, herons, ducks, and geese. Once the trout grow up, they have few predators compared to ocean-going salmon, which must run the gauntlet from seals to killer whales to gill nets, pollution, trollers, dams, and sport fishermen. While a few of the Klamath trout are brown trout, most of them are wild, native rainbows—and they are very wily.

To an angler, the prospect of hooking a trout the size of a salmon on a fly is both exciting and daunting. Fishing on the lake itself is difficult as the water is wide and the fish mercurial. In the summer months the water in the lake warms up and trout seek colder waters, moving up into the inlet rivers at the upper end of the lake. Sometimes the fish swim miles up Williamson River or Wood River or Crystal Creek to find the cold, spring-fed waters there. I have fished Spring Creek, a tributary of the Williamson. I can attest that the water temperature in that creek is, indeed, cold for I waded deep into those waters, and while the air temperature was warm, the water temperature was not. It is there, in those cold waters, where the fish congregate and spawn.

Some trout go directly from Upper Klamath Lake into the Williamson. Farther north other fish swim up the lake through a channel and into Agency Lake and then up that lake's major inlet, the Wood River. The Wood is a winding, cold stream flanked by grasses and weeds taller than a man standing on a stepladder. My friend Dick and I fished there not too long ago, and we had planned to unload the boat at a ramp on Agency Lake. Then we planned to motor up the lake, find the mouth of the Wood, go upriver a few miles, and then later float downriver and fish back to the mouth. But I must tell you about what happened next, in the early morning before we could launch the boat.

The ramp and dock was part of a "resort" on the eastern shore of Agency Lake. Dick and I were the only guests at the resort. Our accommodation was a piece of ground upon which we pitched our tents near a picnic table. The restrooms (running water and flush toilets provided) were nearby as were a handful of empty cabins. The proprietors were a friendly older couple and the faded "For Sale" sign on the property had been there for some time. The boat ramp and dock had apparently been constructed about the same time as the cabins. The ramp's surface was sand and not concrete and you had to be careful, because if you backed the trailer down too far, the wheels of the trailer would drop into a hole and you would have a hell of a time pulling it back out. I know that is true because one time I did back the trailer down too far and it did drop into a hole and I did have a hell of a time pulling it back out.

On that morning we awoke early to go fishing because the weather was promising to be hot and we wanted to get back in the shade by noon. We had a quick breakfast, grabbed our rods and gear, and walked down to the ramp. It was deserted and absolutely quiet in the weak light of the metallic gray dawn. The lake began to wake up and the birds along the reeded shore started to ruffle their wings and began to sing their ancient songs. The silent lake was windless and as smooth as a newly waxed Buick. But all of a sudden I heard a buzzing sound. I looked around and noticed that no one else was around, not even any traffic noise on the paved road that skirted the lake. I looked overhead expecting to see a high-voltage transmission line somewhere and its telltale electric humming sound. As a Pacific Northwest resident, I have seen those husky steel transmission towers marching across the terrain, such as where I used to go chukar hunting in the canyons of the Deschutes and John Day Rivers. Usually, there is a loud humming or buzzing noise that can be unnerving when you get close to those high-voltage wires: thousands of kilowatts running through the lines from the powerhouse at Bonneville Dam to the substations in Los Angeles.

"What's the buzz?" I asked Dick. He shrugged his shoulders.

I looked from one side to the other and did not see any transmission lines, just a standard-issue power line and wooden telephone poles strung along the lonely county road. Then I looked out some twenty yards away from the dock, and there was a dark funnel that spiraled up more than one hundred feet in the air. I had never seen a tornado before, but this was about as close as I imagined that a tornado would be—except that there was no wind. There was not even a ripple on the lake's surface: mirror flat, placid, shimmering, reflecting the dawn's light.

Dick and I gingerly walked out onto the dock and stared at the so-called tornado and realized that it was not a real tornado: It was a tornado of bugs—thousands upon thousands of them buzzing around. The closer we got to the dark funnel, the louder was the sound. We got close enough to grab a few bugs.

"Midges!" said Dick. Or buzzers as the Brits say.

It was only much later that we learned that this apparent explosion of midges was, in fact, a mating swarm of male midges. The female midges hover around the edge of the swarm and now and again dart into the swarm. The male midges have a feathery antenna by which to detect the wing-beat frequency of a female of the same species, and like-species want to mate with their own kind. And they do.

Back then I knew nothing about the mating behavior of the dark funnel of midges that we saw. All we knew was that the buzzing sound was due to flying midges—lots of them. As fly fishermen, we both knew a bit about midges, because midges account for a large share of a trout's diet on streams and especially on lakes. According to the experts, the family *Chironomidae*, commonly called midges, belong to the order *Diptera* or true flies, which includes mosquitoes, no-see-ums, gnats, and others—a thousand-plus species. These midges hatch out of their tiny eggs in the mud and wiggle around eating algae and detritus on the bottom of lakes and slow-moving sections of rivers. Before too long they pupate, rise to the surface, discover that they have wings, and then they fly away. Like spawning salmon, midges stop eating once they focus on reproduction, and within a few days they mate, drop their eggs on or under the water, and then die. Trout are most likely to feed on midges when they are pupating, as they are scurrying around just off the bottom preparing to ascend up to the surface.

These delicate slender insects are usually very small, around size 16 to 22 and smaller, though some are as large as a size 10, especially in Canada. Colors range from black to red, green, and cream. Unlike most aquatic insects, they have only two wings. While they are similar in many ways to mosquitoes in shape and size, *Chironomid* midges do not bite. In fact, midges are called blind mosquitoes by some in the South because they are a mosquito-like insect without the bite.

Still, midges can be a nuisance. The previous day some other guests had arrived late in the day at the resort and apparently one of them did not turn off the lights at night in the men's restroom. That person also had failed to close the outside door when he left. Like moths, midges are attracted to light, and with the restroom lit up like a beacon all night long, in the morning the midges were plastered by the hundreds all over the restroom walls, doors, stalls, and everything else.

Soon the midge swarm dissipated, the mating done for another day. We collected some of the midges and carefully examined them: They were light green and yellow and they were fairly large for a midge, about a size 12. Of course, we had no midge flies that large in our fly boxes, nor did we have the right color. No wonder our midge fishing the day before had been slow.

We put our gear into the boat, cast off from the dock, cranked up the outboard, and headed out to the lake, which was unruffled, seemingly still asleep. We were heading to the mouth of the Wood but we were not exactly sure where the entrance was. As we got closer to the marshy shoreline, I throttled the engine down and we searched for an opening in the reeds. We boated up one inlet, and as it closed in on us, the bottom got shallow. There did not appear to be any current to the thin water, but we pushed a bit farther until I finally shut off the engine and tilted up the motor because we were down to less than a foot deep. I grabbed the oars and rowed a bit farther, and then we turned around and rowed back out of the inlet until we could crank up the motor again.

At the next inlet we also motored up into the marsh, but the water closed in quickly and again we had to shut off the engine. I grabbed the oars and rowed farther into the inlet but could not locate the river's mouth either. So we turned around and went back out into the lake again and continued our search. By then the sun was well up over the horizon, and I was unhappy as I wanted our morning to include some serious fishing and not just exploring.

"Where in the hell is the mouth?" I asked myself as the motor hummed along searching for a break in the shoreline. Dick and I were not the only navigators to discover that finding a river's mouth in a marshy delta can be difficult. La Salle, the famous French explorer, had this problem, too.

In 1682 La Salle traveled down the Mississippi River from the Great Lakes area to the mouth and then he returned to France. While he was not the first European to have seen the river's mouth, La Salle wanted to claim the area as French. So did King Louis XIV, and he directed La Salle to outfit another expedition to establish a small French colony at the mouth of the Mississippi to challenge the Spanish and English in that area. The ill-fated 1684 expedition had trouble with shipwrecks, storms, and a gross misunderstanding of geography, for instead of sighting landfall at the mouth of the Mississippi, they found themselves in Matagorda Bay in Texas some five hundred miles to the west. This miscalculation proved fatal. After several years of unsuccessfully trying to find the mouth of the Mississippi, La Salle was killed by some mutineers near the Brazos River in 1687. A little later the last of the French colonists were killed by Indians, except for perhaps a few children who may have been adopted by some of the Indians.

Our reconnoitering along the north shore of Agency Lake seeking the mouth of Wood River was not likely to be fatal, but it was discouraging. We cruised along the shore trying to find an opening in the tall marsh reeds and grasses. The sun got higher and higher and we wanted to get going, run up the river, and start fishing before the day got blistering hot.

Finally, I noticed a tall, weathered post (with no signage whatsoever) standing up along the edge of the marsh. We got closer and then I found an old white buoy floating on its side in the water attached to an anchor or a log or something heavy. There was a good current flowing around the buoy, but the sandy bottom was shallow and soon we had to shut off the motor again. We rowed up against the current and over onto the bar. We got out of the boat and dragged the boat over the last few feet of the bar. Soon after that we found a channel about three to four feet deep and we got back in the boat, started up the motor, and headed upriver. As the tall reeds closed in on each side of the river, I began feeling claustrophobic: I could see nothing but the river, the bankside reeds, and the blue sky overhead. Dick was standing in the bow searching for the deepest channel of the river, his arms pointing right or left signaling to me so I could maneuver and not run aground. One time the propeller on the outboard hit a submerged log and the engine stopped. Thankfully, the object was only some rotten wood and not a boulder, and so I cranked up the Mercury and we were back in business.

There was no one else on the river that day, and as we penetrated deeper and deeper into the marsh, I felt as though I was Humphrey Bogart as Captain Charlie Allnut piloting the tramp steamer *African Queen* up through the maze of marshland-infested channels trying to reach the open waters of Lake Tanganyika. The *African Queen* was a far cry from my fiberglass drift boat and little outboard motor, but the marsh and water and the inability to see anything on either side of the river was similar. The movie's finest scene, to me, was an overhead shot of the *African Queen*, seemingly adrift in an endless marsh as the captain and his passenger were asleep and exhausted. But as they slept, the rain fell and the water rose, and the boat floated out onto the open lake.

After about two river miles, we stopped and then started to drift back down the river to fish. Sometimes we got out of the boat and fished from the muddy bank. At other times one of us would man the oars and guide the boat down the river and the other one would stand in the bow and cast out ahead. And at other times we would anchor and both of us would cast out of the boat. I would like to report that we caught a couple of two-footers, but that would be untrue. We saw some rises that appeared to be large fish, but the only fish we hooked were smaller trout, around one-footers. We used a variety of flies from mayfly adults to nymphs, from brown leeches to black ones, from large streamers to small ones. We used floating lines and sinking lines. On the retrieval we used the short twitch-twitch method, the long twitch–twitch method, the twitch-pause-twitch method, and the twitch-twitch–pause method, all without success. We saw only one other boat on the river, so the fishing grounds were far from crowded. We saw herons and bitterns and the comical pelicans, as well.

The day got warmer and warmer, but the water itself remained surprisingly cold and clear and the bottom was covered with gravel and sand. We drifted down the river, back into the lake, and then we motored back to the ramp. We put the boat back on the trailer, broke camp, and drove around to the edge of the upper end of Agency Lake. We crossed a little bridge on the Wood River where the river wound through the marshes and then through the pasturelands. Farther still upriver the forest closed in around the banks of the river. Beyond that was the seminal spring that bubbled out of the earth, the fount of the Wood.

To the west of the Wood River is Pelican Bay, the northwest corner of Upper Klamath Lake. Another spring-fed river called Crystal Creek flows into the bay, and that is where the trout congregate in the summer. We camped at a spot not too far away and the next day we drove down to the ramp. We had a real concrete ramp there and that was a delight. The bay was the size of most lakes and we thoughtlessly headed straight out into it. Before long I noticed that the wake behind the boat was brown. We were far from shore but I looked down and realized that the muddy bottom was very shallow, nothing but soft mud. If you got out of the boat and tried to wade, your legs (and maybe all of you) would vanish into the porous mud. I realized that the propeller was churning away through the soft mud, so I shut off the engine and put the oars to work.

"Where's the channel?" I asked Dick.

"I don't know," he said as we both looked around. I finally noticed that there were some buoys on the ramp side of the bay. We saw a large boat as it motored away from the ramp and I watched where it went. Then I saw another boat go in the opposite direction and I watched where it went. Before long I realized that those colored buoys marked the channel.

Dunderheads! Anyway, we rowed toward the buoys and finally reached the channel.

All morning long we cast our various offerings out onto the water. We trolled. We drifted with the wind. We anchored-up. We tied on silvery-colored baitfish with dumbbell red eyes. We tied on damselfly nymphs. We tied on leeches. After several hours we had little to show, except that we spied a few very large trout as they ghosted through the weeds near the shore. I was distracted a bit because the noontime sun bore down on the two of us in the open boat. There was no shade there whatsoever, but I did have an old umbrella in the boat. I grabbed it and I opened it up and instant shade; the sun, mercifully, was off my overheated back.

I went back to searching the shallow water and we both noticed more large rises along the shore. A few of the fish jumped right out of the water and inhaled something, maybe a flying insect? Those leaping fish were trophy-sized trout. We were all eyes. We studied the surface of the water looking for a hatch, but found few bugs on the water, just a few damselflies flying about in the air. We looked closer and speculated that the fish were taking the damselflies right out of the air. Could that be true?

Yes, because suddenly I saw a large rainbow jump all the way out of the water and nail a big, skinny, neon-blue-colored damselfly that was hovering in the air.

"So that's what they're taking," I said.

Damselfly nymphs are one of the basic patterns on fly-fishing lakes, but adult damselflies? Well, Dick happened to have a dry fly somewhat similar to an adult damselfly and he tied it on. I cannot recall what I tied on, but it was something dainty as those slender adult damselflies are about as dainty as can be. We both cast out our offerings the best we could. The water was dead calm, about four feet deep with a few wavy weeds rising all the way up to the surface.

"Damn it's hot!" I mumbled to Dick. I was thinking of reeling in my line and going back to the ramp to rest in the shade.

At the same moment Dick's rod bowed and a huge trout with a pink-colored stripe along its lateral line jumped out of the water and almost landed in the boat.

"Kersplash!"

The leaping fish looked like a coho salmon weighing at least ten pounds, deep-bodied and blindingly brilliant. But it was not a salmon: It was a resident rainbow trout.

Dick reared back on the rod handle and let the fish run—which it did, slicing its way through the languid noonday water, the reel singing as the line ripped off the spool. Finally, we were onto it . . . a two-footer . . . at least two feet . . . probably larger . . . what a fish!

And then . . . well . . . suddenly . . . the line went slack. I looked out where the fish had just been, jumping out of the water, where that wide-bodied bolt of silver catapulted out of the water and into the air, where that powerhouse was tearing line out into the vastness of the bay, where my eyelids were wildly wide open. The space surrounding us simply vanished, nothing but a void, just a dustless vacuum. The time-space continuum had collapsed. The oxygen had been sucked right out of our little world because the fish was G-O-N-E. When we finally re-discovered our vocal cords, our first words were exclamatory and R-rated. And then Dick—a proficient trout fly angler for more than three decades—simply said:

"That's the biggest trout I've ever seen!"

Dick reeled in the line and saw that the fly was intact. The fish had apparently just pulled the hook out of its mouth. We both cast out again. We waited. And we waited. Another ten minutes passed and we noticed that the hatch apparently was over. The rises were gone; the big fish probably scooted their way back down into the deeper waters for we no longer saw any of them, nothing but clear, cool water, weeds weaving through the light-green-colored lake water.

The sun was not any cooler and my water bottle was empty. High noon can be a hot place on the water in the summer. High noon has little subtlety to it, the light intense, the colors washed out by the angle of the sun directly overhead, the long shadows of the morning no longer long, the features of the world stark and gaunt, the shadings gone, a noontime glare, harsh and unforgiving. High noon accompanies the accoutrements you need to survive: dark glasses, sunscreen, hat, thin cotton long-sleeved shirt, and a red bandana that you dip into the lake from time to time and then tie around your neck to cool off. High noon is the noon whistle at the shipyard in Seattle when it is time to take off your work gloves and pick up your lunch pail. High noon is not a time of confrontation as it is in the movies: It is a time of retreat, and we gladly complied.

I pulled the starter rope on the outboard and put it in forward gear. I pulled at the drawstring of my broad-brimmed hat that was fastened around my chin. The rush of the wind was refreshing as the boat zipped along. At the dock I hoped to tie up the boat quickly, throw out the fenders, get in the car, and drive back to the camp. There I would hope to find a lonely shadow or two among the pines where I could put my folding chair down on the ground, a ground hard and cracked after weeks of a rainless sky. I would open a cold bottle of beer and rummage through the ice cooler for sandwich makings. Life would be good, in the shade, satiated with drink and food, a wisp of coolness to the breeze, my boots toppled over on the ground, my bare feet slipping into a pair of flip-flops, my hat off, its leather sweatband soaked. And I would look back at the lake and the fishing and the excitement and I would think to myself that yes, we had our glimpse of a two-footer on the line—but my, oh, my, wasn't it all too brief?

Chapter Eleven

Of Shasta, Bats, and Goldens

Mount Shasta towers over the Klamath River plateau, dominating across the wide plain of northern California where it can be seen hundreds of miles away. I have seen that mountain many times over many decades and it never ceases to surprise me—suddenly out on that lean, high-elevation plain appears a broad-shouldered, white-sheathed volcano, shimmering in the California sun, all alone, no cities nearby, the two-lane highway stretching out into the dryness of a summer day, scrawny pines dotting a blanket of withered grass and sagebrush.

Perhaps the best view I ever had of Mount Shasta was on an Amtrak train traveling from Portland to San Francisco. The night train coursed its way through the Cascades and I woke up very early in the still-dark morning. The coach had only a few lights illuminated because most of the passengers were sleeping or at least trying to sleep. I had looked out the window earlier in the night and seen nothing but blackness for we were in the mountains and the area was lightly populated with no towns or electric lights, a dark sky if ever there was one. All I could see was my own reflection.

But this time I looked out the window and was startled to see a broadside view of Mount Shasta right in front of me, flooded with light, a moonlight brightness reflecting on the mountain's newly fallen snow. I could not see the moon itself due to the steep terrain, but it must have been a full moon because the snowfields and glaciers of the mountain were absolutely aglow, not a sunny type of glow, but a ghostly glow for moonlight is always pale, incapable of glowing, not alive like the furnace of the sun, but reflective and passive. I stared at the mountain and tried to drink it in, but the train clicked its way along and soon the mountain was gone from my view. The coach once again was darkened; I shifted about in my seat, put my coat around my shoulders, and tried to get back to sleep.

Mount Shasta and its nearby companion, Mount Lassen, lie at the southern terminus of the Cascade Range. Mount Shasta is only 250 feet less in elevation than Mount Rainier, and like many of the Cascade volcanoes, it is expected to erupt again—we just do not know when. Despite its symmetrically cone-shaped snowy mountain, Mount Shasta has erupted many times over thousands of years, the last time about two hundred years ago. Like Mount Hood, mountaineers attempt to climb Mount Shasta by the thousands every year and many succeed. And unlike the other Cascade peaks, Mount Shasta is the only major Cascade mountain that has an Indian name. The name "Shasta" refers to the Shasta tribe that has lived in the Klamath River tributaries around the Yreka area for millennia. Other nearby tribes include the Klamath tribe and the Modoc tribe.

The waters from the slopes of Mount Shasta flow into the Klamath River to the north and the Sacramento River to the south. Like the Deschutes River headwaters, the slopes of Mount Shasta are veined with underground springs, for it is a land of lava. The surface and sub-surface waters to the south of the mountain are the headwaters of the Sacramento, the second-largest river on the West Coast. While the Klamath River courses its way through both California and Oregon, the Sacramento watershed is almost entirely within the boundary of the state of California. At some point around Mount Lassen, the Cascades leave the basalt, volcanic terrain behind and emerge as a land of granite known as the Sierras. The Sacramento's major tributaries include the McCloud and Pit Rivers to the north and the Feather and American Rivers to the east.

The first Europeans who saw the Sacramento River were English-speaking explorers from the north and Spaniards from the south. In 1808 a Spanish army officer and explorer, Gabriel Moraga, ventured up from San Francisco Bay to the delta and saw a large river flowing down from the north. He named the river the *Rio de los Sacramentos*

(River of the Sacraments). Later the name was anglicized and shortened to the Sacramento River.

The first man who saw the northern reaches of the Sacramento apparently was Peter Skene Ogden, the Canadian-born adventurer who led a number of exploratory trips in the West under the direction of the British Hudson's Bay Company. It is unclear quite how far south Ogden went on his 1827 trip, but he claimed that he saw Mount Shasta and thereby the Sacramento's headwaters. Ogden, and the fur trappers who came after him, had crossed the border from Oregon country to Alta California, Mexican territory, but that did not seem to bother them. The ensuing history of northern California is familiar with the change in governments, the Gold Rush, logging, commerce, increasingly intensive agriculture, and the state's hydrological re-plumbing. Before long nearly all of the Sacramento and its major tributaries had been blocked by dams.

The largest dam on the river, Shasta Dam, was built during World War II, and it is the second-largest dam in mass in the country, right behind Grand Coulee. Some six hundred feet high and almost 550 feet at the base, the dam backs up the Sacramento, McCloud, and Pit Rivers and creates the state's largest reservoir. The dam generates hydroelectricity and rations out irrigation water to the south. The dam blocked the river's upper salmon spawning waters, but most of the resident trout have persevered.

It is that area, upstream of the dam's reservoir, that I have found to be a splendid place: the "Upper Sac" and its tributaries, with its clean, cold water, its rugged canyon difficult for anglers and hikers alike, and its trout ever tempting. The Upper Sac flows out of the flanks of Mount Shasta with its lava-fired landscape. It is a hurry-up river gushing its way down the mountain. The whitewater river is cleaved by the twisted mountains and it runs along a north-south transportation corridor for both the railroad and Interstate 5. The Upper Sac is a narrow area from the streambed to the steep hillsides, and it is unclear whether it should be called a ravine or a canyon. Between the headwaters of the mountain and the slack water of the reservoir are little tributaries like Shotgun Creek, Flume Creek, Soda Creek, and Salt Creek.

Two large tributaries flow into the reservoir: the McCloud and Pit Rivers. The McCloud is only some eighty miles long but its waters are especially cold and clean. The Pit is a longer river, some two hundred miles long, and its watershed reaches all the way into southern Oregon. Before the damming of Shasta Dam and its reservoir, the annual flow of the Pit River was greater than that of the Sacramento at the confluence of the two rivers. Now the lower reaches of the Pit, the McCloud, and the Upper Sac are all inundated by the reservoir. The Pit is named for the pitfall traps that the local Indians dug to capture game. Like the Klamath and Columbia, the Pit cuts through the Cascades and has a series of hydroelectric dams along its path. For some reason the hydro planners were short on words because they named the dams numerically, in contrast to most other dams, such as Iron Gate Dam on the Klamath or McNary Dam on the Columbia or Ice Harbor Dam on the Snake. As a result, the hydroelectric dam system on the Pit River is unceremoniously referred to as Pit Dam 3, Pit Dam 4, and Pit Dam 5.

Most of my fishing over the years in that Mount Shasta area has been on the Upper Sac and McCloud, although I did fish the Pit River one time and found it one of the most difficult rivers I have ever waded. I cannot tell you exactly where my Californian friend Bill and I fished on the Pit, but the places we went were nearly impassable. At the time I was not feeling well due to a lingering illness, so I was not quite up to snuff and I found the going very tough: It took me more than two hours to wade and fish about one hundred yards of stream bank. The word *bank* was a misnomer on that river because there was no actual bank or shoreline. The water spread out thinly for more than twenty feet beyond the main channel. The flat rocky terrain was pockmarked with good-sized holes and covered with large-leafed watery plants. Each step was a mystery: You might put your wading boot down in two inches deep of water or you might end up having your foot, and your leg, too, tumble down into a watery hole.

I continued on the best I could. It was late in the afternoon on a mid-June day and the bugs were out. When I finally could get to where I wanted to go, I cast out onto the water and soon had some strikes. The rainbows that I hooked had been taken on a medium-sized dark caddis, and later I tied on a little yellow stone. The golden stoneflies were already gone. I would have liked to have fished longer as the evening was ahead of us and the river was not crowded, but I was tiring quickly. With my illness still plaguing me, I found the wading exhausting, and eventually, I climbed back up the steep bank to the road. Bill came along shortly and we drove back to camp.

I have not been back to the Pit, for I am older now and do not think I would do any better now than I did then. Instead, I have spent my time on the Upper Sac itself and the McCloud over the years with Bill and another California friend named Don. I have known both of them since we were boys living alongside of the banks of the Columbia River. For decades our rendezvous has been a Forest Service campground on the Upper Sac. The trips have a sameness to them: I drive into camp along the far side of the river and it seems exactly the same as it did the year before and the year before that. I get out of the car and Bill and Don are setting up their tents. They look much the same, a bit less hair on their heads and a bit more gray too, but otherwise not much different than when we were all cavorting on the banks of the Columbia wearing cut-off jeans and Converse sneakers.

Memory and eyesight can get tangled up because the image in my mind's eye does not reflect the image in my eye's eye. In my eye's eye I see a couple of aging men, maybe not old but not young either. By contrast, my mind's eye sees a couple of teenagers off on yet another lark. The mind's eye is blind to the men in real time who are staking down their tents, men who have not been on a lark but who have been working for decades, men with wives and children and grandchildren and who have experienced illnesses and sorrow and joy. The camp's mix of pines and oaks and madrone alongside the freestone river melds together with our voices and our presence. When you go back to a place time and time again, the place and the people merge into memory. And then one time you come back alone and see the place and you look for them and maybe they are not there and someday they will never be there again, but they will be there in another way, as ghosts, invisible, mindful images infused into the place. Such is a place alongside the waters, not just a three-dimensional place but more so, a place that contains something more than a piece of ground and its waters, but time as well.

Both the Upper Sac and the McCloud are walk-and-wade rivers because a drift boat would be unnavigable there. While the wading may not be as arduous as on the Pit, it is nonetheless not easy. Just getting down to the river can be a challenge with the steep rocky banks, poison oak spreading its way along the ground, and a jungle of brush where you try to thread your way to the river using the sound of the river because you cannot see the water due to the thick foliage. I recall one time that Don and I spent too long fishing in the evening and had to hike back up a steep bank in the dark. The gravel was loose, the felt-soled wading boots were smooth, and the blackberry vines reached out to prick you at any movement. I was lucky and escaped up to the road unscathed, but Don was not as fortunate and those vines did a good job of shredding his waders.

On the Upper Sac most fly anglers pay close attention to the two seminal fly fishermen in that country: the late Ted Fay and the late Joe Kimsey. Those two anglers pioneered the "high-stick" method of dropping nymphs down very quickly into the Upper Sac's pocket water. The idea is to wade in close to a likely spot, use a short line, and pinch a split-shot a foot or two above the fly. Then lob that assemblage out into the water close to the pocket, maybe just below a good-sized boulder. Keep your rod high and pay attention to the movement of the leader or strike indicator. The river is usually swift there so you have only a few seconds to put that fly down near the bottom where the trout is resting in the lee of the rock.

Such is my gross summary of the high-stick method. Years ago I actually listened to one of Joe's spontaneous lectures on this subject at his fly shop in Dunsmuir. Among other things he did not think much of strike indicators: just use a bit of fingernail paint on the upper end of the leader and then pay close attention to how that leader curls and moves. The movement of the leader is critical, because by the time you actually feel the strike, it's too late to set the hook, said Joe.

I have done quite a bit of high-sticking on the Upper Sac and on other pocket water rivers, too, and yes, it does work. But like many fly anglers, I really like top-water action, and what I especially like about the Upper Sac, and the McCloud, are the evening hatches. Almost every time I have been in that country, I have found some type of insect activity in the evening: golden stones, little yellow stones, several types of caddis, pale evening duns, and more. Of course, just because there are bugs in the air does not necessarily mean that the fish are on to it. Sometimes they are and sometimes they are not.

In addition to those evening bug hatches, there is another type of winged creature on the Upper Sac—and on some other rivers—that is of importance to fly anglers, too. Bats. Most fly-fishing anglers have at one time or another encountered bats flying about on the river at dusk. Occasionally, bats have bumped into anglers in the dim light of the evening, and a few anglers have actually been bitten by a bat. Certainly, bats are wonderful animals and they help reduce insect pests, such as mosquitoes. And other than Dumbo, bats are the only mammals that are able to fly. Still, I am not enamored with bats.

I remember wading on the Upper Sac not too many years ago. A lively mayfly hatch was getting downright wooly, rises were all over the river, and my #14 Pale Morning Dun (PMD) was getting pecked at by some nice rainbows. Suddenly, a bat zipped by me overhead. Five minutes later came another bat, low in under the radar, and it nearly hit me in the torso. When you are up to your butt in a river, you don't move quickly. I ducked awkwardly to avoid the bat and nearly lost my balance. Thankfully, I was using my wading staff or I probably would have gone down.

I had always thought that bats would never run into a human because of their sensitive echolocation, or bio-sonar, whereby they are able to find flying insects in the dead of night. Moreover, the old saying, "blind as a bat," is untrue because bats have perfectly good eyesight. Despite their eyesight and echolocation, bats still bump into people from time to time— usually those people are fly anglers because who else other than anglers wade about in the river hip deep at dusk? We fly anglers not only wade around in the river while the bats are flying, but we also cast our artificial flies around in the air. If we are halfway decent fly tiers, those artificial flies should closely resemble real bugs. Bats catch and eat insects and they are very good at it. They scoop the bugs up into their webbing and then pick the bugs up and put them into their mouths.

The light was dim and getting dimmer on the Upper Sac, and I could see those little aerial mammals all over the river—darting dark spots against a dusky sky. Every now and again a bat would swoop in and try to catch my fly as I cast it out into the air. Fortunately, the bat did not nail my PMD, but I have talked to other anglers who have experienced just that.

And then what happens?

When you have a bat on your line—instead of a fish—you are in trouble. A friend of mine had this experience once, and he said that in the low light of the evening he noticed that something was hung up on the end of the line. He thought it was a branch or a little glob of some debris. He reeled in the line, reached over, and grabbed onto whatever-it-was.

"Yikes!"

Whatever-it-was, in fact, was a bat, and the bat bit my friend on the hand. Bats can have rabies, a viral infection that if not treated attacks the brain and nervous system and likely will kill you. Most bats do not have rabies, but just in case, the prudent person should be careful if they have been bitten by a bat. If possible, they should kill the bat and send it to a hospital lab. There an autopsy on the bat's brain tissue can determine whether or not the bat has rabies. If the bat does not have rabies, you are home free. If it does have rabies, you get to have a series of unpleasant vaccine shots. If a bat bites you and you do not send the specimen to the lab or if it flies away, well, you might want to get the vaccination, just to be safe.

After another twenty minutes on the Upper Sac, I waded back to shore because the twilight was gone and it was downright dark. The bats and the mayflies both seemed to have flown off into their respective caves or wherever they go. Fortunately, I was not bitten by anything more dangerous than a mosquito. Several bats nearly collided with me, but that was as close as it got. I started hiking up the bank, threading the rod through the hole in the thickly vegetated trail, trying not to get the fly and leader tangled up. At a certain point in the evening, I realized that my eyesight had suddenly gotten weaker and weaker. I felt hesitant, hoping not to stumble, and I kept thinking about bats, even though they were no longer around me. I thought about the fruit bats in Southeast Asia that have a wing-span of five feet. I kept moving . . . looking around from side to side in the dark . . . my mind racing and me thinking way too much about bats.

Over the years most of my attention on those California angling evenings has been focused on bugs, not bats. A strong hatch can be an overwhelming sensation, and I recall once on the McCloud that I experienced an especially prolific hatch. The McCloud is a cold, spring-fed river that flows off the slopes of Mount Shasta. The McCloud drainage is the southern range of the bull trout, or what formerly were called Dolly Varden trout. Those native trout require cold, clean water and generally live in mountain headwaters. They have an olive-green color to them with tiny yellow spots on their backs and red and black spots on their flanks. Their heads are broad and flat. Bull trout once lived in the lower pools of the McCloud and every now and again migrated up into their spawning waters. They grew up to ten pounds and more on a diet of insects, sculpins, juvenile salmon, frogs, and mice. The bull trout population slowly declined after World War II due to the lack of salmon smolts, because the salmon runs were blocked by Shasta Dam. In 1975 the last bull trout was caught, tagged, and released. Most experts speculate that the bull trout in the McCloud are extinct.

It was around the Fourth of July that Bill and I were camping and fishing on the McCloud, looking for rainbow trout. The small camp was close to the river and its water had a haunting turquoise-blue color to it. The gradient was steep so there was a lot of pocket water, riffles, whitewater, and a few pools, too. The wading was tougher than the Upper Sac, but not quite as rigorous as the Pit. The forested terrain was covered with poison oak in many places and we had to be cautious when bushwhacking to the river. The trail out of camp was not just any trail—it was the Pacific Crest Trail that goes from Mexico to Canada. The McCloud section of the Crest Trail was an easy hike for us as we moved along the path until we had to leave it and go overland down to the river. The brush was thick and interspersed with boulders and driftwood tangles next to the bank. Once I got into the river, the water was ice cold and my waders were a must, even when the weather was hot.

I tied on a Prince nymph and did some high-sticking in the little calm spots in the rushing current of the McCloud. I dropped my line into a back eddy, where the current went contrary to the main flow. Later I lobbed my nymph and split-shot just downstream of a boulder and in its lee there appeared to be a calm spot where a fish could rest and look at the morsels of food as they drifted by. As the current continued downriver of the boulder, its flow slowed and began to pile up, forming a mound, almost breaking the surface. Over on the far side of the river, I noticed another boulder and below it the water piled up there, too; the mound grew taller and taller, eventually creating a crest that then toppled over into a spray of white foam. Then farther downriver I saw a riffle and thought I might cast out into it, but I first decided to take off the split-shot as the water was no longer deep. Riffles are shallow areas where a strong current flows along a coarse riverbed. Oftentimes the fish like to lie in those riffles where the dislodged bugs drift by—a moving smorgasbord. But the promising riffle did not pan out: My offering was not accepted and I continued wading downstream from one spot to the next. The permutations of flowing water over rocks are endless—just as are the number of places a trout might want to hide.

Eventually, I got out of the water and hiked back to camp for lunch. During the afternoon the sun was out and the weather was perfect, warm but not uncomfortably hot. The monarch butterflies were flying about, their fluttering, moth-like flight unlike the flight of the winged aquatic insects. Another smaller type of butterfly flew by and then another. I had no idea what they were, but later I learned that they were called the California Sister butterfly. Its upper body was colored dark gray with white bands and orange patches near the tips of the forewings. The underside has a different coloration with browns, blues, oranges, and whites. I was taken by the intricate design of the California Sister, even though I usually do not pay much attention to insects other than the aquatic types. Most other people are just the opposite when it comes to entomology: They are awed by a butterfly, its coloration, its dainty flight, its ethereal lightness, but those same people are largely ignorant about aquatic insects. Aside from honeybees, I cannot think of a more benevolent and popular insect in the insect world than butterflies. A number of states have an official state butterfly—and by the way, the California Sister butterfly is not that state's official butterfly; it is the California dogface butterfly.

In the evening the sun was low and the butterflies were long gone, and instead of hiking back up the trail to fish, I walked down below camp as there was a nice run there with a tempting far bank that had an overhang of watery plants, their huge leaves touching down to the river's edge. The trout often like to hang in under the protection of such leaves, like an awning above a city sidewalk. Sometimes the fish like to lie in right along the edge of the leaves or the grasses and scan the surface for dead or dying insects as they float by. The McCloud and the Upper Sac have a lot of this type of water—good dry-fly fishing.

We were in a deep canyon so the sun disappeared early on, but the twilight continued for hours. On these waters it is never quite certain what type of hatch may appear—if any. In this case it was the tail end of the golden stonefly hatch, and those large, yellow-golden bugs started to fill the air. The river was not wide, the banks were treed, and the hillsides were steep and rising ever upward: a mountainous and rugged place. I was wading in knee-deep water bordered with trees on both sides. Into this space above the surface of the river were thousands of cubic feet of air, and it was no longer comprised of simply atmospheric gases, dust, and pollens; it was also filled with thousands of fluttering golden stones, not like the graceful flight of the mayfly, but something almost comical, as though stoneflies have too many wings on their bodies—or maybe not enough. Regardless of their lack of grace, the air was filled with them.

The female golden stones hovered above the surface of the river. At times I could see their tiny eggs falling out of their abdomens, the eggs plopping down into the river, drifting down into the flow, drifting down into the crevices of the gravel. There the eggs would incubate in the cold, clean water and emerge as nymphs. Golden stones grow for as long as two years and get quite large for an insect, more than an inch long. They have two antennae and two tails. The color of the nymph is darker than the adult, more a light-tan to brown color. Cold water entrains more oxygen than warmer water, and stoneflies thrive in such areas because the McCloud is a very cold river: When I have waded deep for some time, I usually end up shivering despite the warmth of a summer's day. Eventually, the nymphs use their six jointed legs efficiently and crawl slowly across the bottom of the riverbed, emerge on land, and shed their exoskeletons, letting their membranous veined wings dry in the air. After drying their wings they soon mate, sometimes on the blades of the grasses or sometimes in the tree branches. They fly around for a few days, oviposit, and die. Goldens, and most other stoneflies, are clumsy fliers and fall into the water often, much to the delight of the waiting trout.

As the evening darkened, the very air glowed, the goldens fluttering to beat the band from bank to bank, from the river's surface up into the sky; they were so thick they must have had trouble avoiding midair collisions. There must have been thousands of them up and down the slick in front of me. They would fall into the water, float for a few feet downstream, and then there would be a big splash. As nymphs, they were comfortable in the water, but as air-breathing, winged adults, they found themselves helpless in the water, flopping around aimlessly, their pathetic wingbeats getting weaker by the minute, unable to right themselves, unable to re-launch themselves back into the safety of the air.

I, of course, had an adult golden stonefly on the tippet, and I put some floatant gel on the fly's body and wings. I cast out on the far side near the edge of the foliage and then watched the fly float by, trying to keep my line mending to avoid any drag. Sometimes nothing would happen and I would cast out again. Other times a fish would slap at it but not really bite down on it. I had many more such strikes than I had "real" strikes, the ones that put steel to lip. Every now and again a handsome rainbow came to hand, some measuring up to fourteen inches or so, strong and healthy.

The fish seemed to be in an absolute frenzy and it was contagious because I got frantic myself, especially as the light was going fast; the forested banks on either side were already dark. This type of hatch does not happen every day. I looked downriver and I saw Bill casting and casting again; he must have been in the zone, too. I inadvertently snapped the fly off on an overhanging tree branch and had to tie on another one. It was nearly dark and I had a terrible time trying to thread the tippet through the eye of the hook. My fingers were shaking and I was not sure if it was due to the cold water that I was standing in or the frenzy of the hatch. I put my magnifying glasses on and tried to thread the tippet through the eye of the hook again. I still could not do it. I picked up my tiny flashlight, about the size of a cigarette. I turned it on, clamped it down between my teeth, and held it tight while the beam of light illuminated the fly. Thankfully, the fly was relatively large and so I was able to finally stick the tippet through the eye, tie it, bear down on the improved clinch knot, and clip the tag. Then I fumbled around trying to figure out where in the hell the floatant was. It was not in the usual spot.

"This is taking *way* too long!" I grumbled to myself. Exasperated and shivering, at last I finally found the gel and greased up the fly. Time waits for no man.

As I waded back into the river ready to cast, I noticed that there were fewer bugs in the air, and I was not seeing any splashes on the water either. Darkness had descended on the face of the waters; the once turquoise-blue water was now black, a reflective sheen in places but still opaque. I no longer saw any fish attacking the goldens as they had just a short time before. Maybe the goldens had flown away from the river to roost on the stalks of the tall grasses for the night. Maybe the trout were satiated, the goldens still wiggling around in the fish's fat gullets. While a golden may be only an inch long, it is a hefty meal for a twelve-inch trout.

I cast out the newly tied golden stone and put it in next to the over-hanging leaves; the fly floated high on the water, buoyant with the gel, and it drifted downstream, ready to be molested by a trout. The fly just kept on going down the current. I pulled the line in and cast it out again. I went at it a couple more times and then reeled in the line, put the fly back in the keeper, and waded back to shore. By then it was dark, indeed, the night flowing in like a black flood.

It had been a good day.

Section IV

The Rockies

CHAPTER TWELVE

Rivers Without Water

THE WATERS OF CALIFORNIA'S TWO LARGEST RIVERS—THE SACRA-mento and the Klamath—flow into the Pacific Ocean, but just to the east is a much larger river that barely flows out into the sea at all. The Colorado River basin comprises parts of seven US states and two Mexican states. Its watershed is almost the same size as the Columbia River basin. In its natural state—more than one hundred years ago—the Colorado had an average discharge of 22,500 cubic feet per second flowing into the Gulf of California, about 10 percent of what the Columbia discharges at its mouth.

But for decades the Colorado's discharge at the mouth has been little more than a trickle. Due to the waterworks over the past century, the Colorado's water is almost totally "utilized" for irrigation, hydropower, municipalities, and industry. The Colorado is one of the most controlled rivers in the world. It is a working river and it courses its way through some of the most stunning canyons in the world, including many national parks. After years of dewatering the Colorado, a 2012 US-Mexican agreement launched an experiment whereby a tiny amount of the river's water will be allowed to flow into the sea at the mouth and help rejuvenate some of the delta's wetlands that have largely dried up.

Still, if the destiny of a river is to empty its waters into the sea, the Colorado River has abdicated its duty. A river is supposed to provide nutrients, freshwater, and marine life to the coastal regions, but that is not the case in the Colorado. The same goes for the Rio Grande, the Colorado's adjacent watershed on the east side of the Continental Divide.

The Rio Grande's watershed includes Colorado, New Mexico, and Texas in the US and four states in Mexico. Yet, after nearly nineteen hundred miles from its headwaters in Colorado's San Juan Mountains to the Gulf of Mexico, you can, at times, wade across the Rio Grande at its mouth. As Will Rogers said: "The Rio Grande is the only river I know of that is in need of irrigating."

Despite the failure of not sending their waters to the sea, both rivers have admirable qualities, especially in their headwaters. Unfortunately, though I have not been able to spend as much time as I would have liked to in those two immense western watersheds, I have visited and fished on several of the rivers in both watersheds. A traveler sees things differently than does a resident, and both perspectives can be useful. I have been a middle-of-the-road type of person when it comes to traveling, especially on the subject of rivers. I recall a story about a British Spey fly-fishing casting instructor who traveled to the West Coast and was flummoxed because the class he was to teach was located on the right-hand side of the river. Apparently, all his fishing had been done on the left-hand side of his favorite British river. On the other hand, I know of some affluent fly fishermen who travel around the globe cherry-picking the finest fishing waters from Brazil to Siberia, from the Caribbean to Iceland. Personally, I think it is important to develop a sense of place where you get to know a river, but at the same time it is invigorating to discover new waters, too.

Some years ago I enjoyed spending a week in Colorado with my elderly father and two brothers. The goal was a ride on the narrow-gauge Durango-Silverton railroad, for my father was a steam-train buff. In route we happened to crisscross the spine of the Continental Divide. Along the way we saw rivers bound to the Gulf of Mexico and others bound to the Gulf of California. Of course, I took my fly-fishing gear along.

The first thing I had to remind myself was that Colorado's mile-high cities and farmlands are higher in elevation than are most of the mountain passes in the Pacific Northwest. Our trip began at the Denver airport, and after picking up a rental car, we headed south along the Front Range and later we went westward. Eventually, we found ourselves one night at a small horse ranch near Salida in the Arkansas River valley surrounding the Sangre de Cristo Mountains. The "valley" was about seven thousand feet and I recall asking our host about how much snow they had in the winter. At that elevation in the Pacific Northwest, the snowfall would be up to the rooftop.

"The snow falls on the fourteeners . . . we don't have much snow left in the valley," our host said.

"Fourteeners?"

"Mountains over fourteen thousand feet," answered our host. Later I learned that Colorado has over fifty of them.

Back down in the valley were the headwaters of the Arkansas River, and I hustled down there later in the afternoon. I was told that the upper Arkansas was good trout water, and I was hoping I might catch a native greenback cutthroat trout. I talked to a ranch hand where we stayed and he was helpful about where I might find a place to fish, for there was a lot of private land that was closed to fishing. Sunburned neck, hands roughened by work, and a cowboy hat on his head, he knew all about that ranch country. He told me that he was fifty years old and had never been outside of the state. He reminded me of a character from Willa Cather's novel *The Song of the Lark* who knew the country "like the blisters on his own hands." As I had only been in the state for three days, I trusted his information and he led me to the river.

I pulled my rental car into a dirt parking lot alongside the river, got out, and strung up my rod. I tied on a small Gold Ribbed Hare's Ear, a good all-around nymph pattern to use when you have no idea what to do. The water was cold and clear. In a few places you could wade across, though I am sure in many other months that would not be possible. Upstream was the river's source near the mining town of Leadville at almost ten thousand feet. Downstream more than a thousand miles away was its confluence with the Mississippi River in the delta farmland of Desha County, Arkansas.

I cast out the nymph and let the weighted fly drop below the surface, and I watched the cold, clean trout water, and thought of the water flowing by hundreds and hundreds of miles through Kansas and Oklahoma and Arkansas, growing cloudy, warming up, the trout gone, the bass robust and later the catfish plentiful, too. At the confluence with the Mississippi, the Arkansas's waters began to weave their way into the fabric of our nation's largest river.

In another time and in another place, I looked out from the deck of a little ferry near Baton Rouge, Louisiana, and thought of those Arkansas River threads as they melded their way into that latte-colored river coursing between the Mississippi's tall levees. My wife and I were in a rental car and the ferry crossing took only fifteen minutes, but they were long minutes and the current was strong, not languid as I had imagined it would be on the Big Muddy. The unforgiving, relentless current was hard up against the old ferry's starboard side; the river's big hydraulics ripped across the current seams and created whirlpools that could suck up a Fiat. Off the port side of the ferry, I imagined that there might be a ninety-pound catfish resting under a bedrock ledge, its eyes looking out as the slurry of entrained sediment shuffled by along the river's bottom.

Back on the upper Arkansas, the river kept flowing by, relentlessly too as all rivers do, but in a benign way, the water clear, the depth no greater than a broomstick. I changed flies once and then twice and finally decided I had better get back to the ranch. I hiked up to the parking lot and put my gear away and looked out at the fine little river that I probably would never see again. It is hard not to ponder when you see a good-looking river flowing by.

As Izaak Walton said in *The Compleat Angler*: "And an ingenious Spaniard says, that 'Rivers and the inhabitants of the watery element were made for wise men to contemplate and fools to pass by without consideration.' And though I will not rank myself in the number of the first, yet give me leave to free myself from the last."

The next day we headed west and south toward Durango and in the process we crossed another major headwater, the mighty Rio Grande, at the town of Del Norte. There the river was not so mighty: Instead it was a wonderful trout stream, its waters bound southward to the New Mexico border and later snaking its way along the border between Texas and Mexico. Upstream of the town the river is designated as a Gold Medal Water where a fly angler might have a decent chance of hooking into a large brown trout. Reportedly, the upper Rio Grande is a fine stonefly river, with the salmonfly hatch ever popular. I wish I could have dipped my line into that water, but I did not have time. Plus, a lot of that ranch country is privately owned and often finding public access to the river can be difficult and time consuming.

After we crossed the bridge, we drove up toward the Continental Divide, toward the two-mile-high Wolf Creek Pass in the San Juan Mountains. The higher in elevation we went, the brighter was the blue of the already blue sky; at the same time the pines thinned out and the trees became shorter and gnarly, twisted by the winter winds. In the folds of the grass-covered hills were the quaking aspen groves, the leaves already starting to turn. As we approached the pass, our rental car went along smoothly, despite the ten thousand feet.

As we descended down from the pass, we entered the Colorado River watershed, where the waters from the high-country creeks flow into the Colorado and eventually go out into the Gulf of California. Before long we came into the handsome city of Durango, and right in the middle of that city was a fine trout river. On the map the river was called the Animas River, although its original name was more lyrical: *El Rio de las Animas* (The River of Lost Souls). The first European to discover the river and name it was Juan de Rivera of Santa Fe, who explored that region in 1765. The surrounding San Juan Mountains are mineral rich, and while Juan de Rivera did not find the Seven Cities of Gold, later American miners extracted a lot of gold and silver in the river's headwaters and they named the nearby town Silverton. Not surprisingly, over the years the lack of environmental controls in the early mining operations polluted the river's tributary creeks and even the river itself. Ordinarily, a river's mountain headwaters are clear and pure, and only later do they grow dirty with the cities and incumbent development, but in this case it was just the reverse.

During our stay in Durango, we took a trip on the Durango & Silverton Narrow Gauge Railroad and Dad was delighted to watch the steam locomotive laboring its way up through the canyon toward Silverton. The track hugged sheer canyon walls along the river, and looking out the window of the coach, I could see the churning rapids and rushing waters below and understood why the Spanish explorers might have named the river as they did.

The active mining areas in the upper reaches of the river had ceased by the early 1990s, and since then efforts to remediate the area have been ongoing. The middle section of the river flows through Durango and it is a popular area for whitewater rafting and fishing. I, too, took my fly rod and gear and went down to the banks of the river. I was hoping to hook a rainbow or maybe a brown trout, both populations apparently robust though neither is native to the state. Somewhere along our trip I was hoping to catch one of Colorado's native cutthroats—such as a greenback cutthroat, yellowfin cutthroat, Rio Grande cutthroat, or a Colorado cutthroat—but they have had a tough time over the years.

I waded out into the river, its banks bordered by city buildings. My fishing journal entries were silent on the types of flies that I tied on that early fall morning. Also, I failed to record any strikes, but all the same I enjoyed fishing on a clear, fast-running river right in town. I am sure the locals had already figured out all the secret spots, but as a newcomer, I was fishing blind. I dimly recall that I hooked a couple of small rainbows in some of the riffle water, but it was not the fish that were memorable to me, it was the river—how snappy and friendly it was as it flowed down through town. The local residents must have been happy to be living in front of their own trout river, for most of us have to drive much farther away for such pleasures. I imagine that the auto parts store clerk or banker or real estate broker might be able to walk down to the banks of the river and throw a line in the water during his lunch hour.

In 2015 a couple of changes were made to the river, one accidental and the other deliberate. The Environmental Protection Agency was investigating the innards of the Gold King Mine in the Silverton headwaters area, specifically assessing the impounded toxic mining wastewater. A plug in that wastewater reservoir was accidentally dislodged and released three million gallons of heavy metals laden with arsenic, cadmium, and lead. The mustard yellow sludge flowed into Cement Creek, an upper tributary of the Animas, and later down the Animas itself. Befouled all the way down to Durango, the spill was news across the country for the once whitewater-rafting, fly-fishing river on the banks of a picturesque western town had become a sewer. A year later the EPA designated the Gold King Mine as a Superfund site and the ongoing cleanup of the toxic-laden sediments—plus the usual litigation—is expected to continue for years.

Also around the same time, the Animas River was altered in another way. A pumping station south of town began pumping some of the Animas water uphill through a six-foot-diameter pipe and into a reservoir. In turn the water in that reservoir now flows down into another watershed. The water engineering project was finally completed after a decades-long, contentious, water-rights controversy involving the Southern Ute tribe located along the Colorado–New Mexico border. As Mark Twain allegedly said about the West: Whiskey is for drinking, water is for fighting.

In the broader sense water is indeed for fighting because water makes life possible on Earth. Other nearby planets and moons have water on them, but not in liquid form. The moons of Saturn and the planet Pluto are believed to be veritable ice balls, encrusted with mantles of ice miles thick. Likewise, Venus may contain water as a gaseous vapor because the temperatures are too hot for liquid water to exist. But on Earth, the Goldilocks planet, we got it just right: not too cold, not too hot.

As for the 126-mile-long Animas, it is unclear what might happen in the years ahead. Its headwaters country begins in the gold and silver veins deep inside the San Juan Mountains, honeycombed with tunnels and little creeks flowing through the canyon. In the middle reaches of the river are the ranchers, rafters, anglers, and those who live and work in Durango. Farther south the river crosses the border into the state of New Mexico. The river eventually flows into the San Juan River, which then turns west. There the river is but a few miles from the intersection of the four big southwestern states where you can bend over and place your hands and feet on all four states at once.

The San Juan continues west bordering the huge Navajo Indian Reservation and dies in the still waters of "Lake" Powell at the confluence of the Colorado River. I have put quotation marks around the word *Lake* because a body of water backed up by a large dam should be called a reservoir and not a lake. And to make matters worse, "Lake" Powell is dedicated to the pioneer scientist and Southwest explorer, John Wesley Powell, who urged the federal government not to build large dams in the arid Southwest. He also urged people not to move water from one basin to another and not to sell trans-basin waters to cities. Instead, he urged farmers to carefully conserve the Southwest water and fund their own small-scale dams and canals within their own respective watersheds. Powell died in 1902. Sixty-one years later the US Bureau of Reclamation built the Glen Canyon Dam and named the reservoir in Powell's name. The reservoir flooded a canyon 180 miles long, creating the second-largest reservoir in the country. Not surprisingly, the largest reservoir in the country is also on the Colorado: It is just downriver and is called "Lake" Mead.

The Glen Canyon Dam appears to be a permanent fixture of the Southwest economy, but that may not be viable in the long run. First, seepage and evaporation has reduced the amount of water available in the reservoir. Second, a river's flow is comprised not only of water, but also of entrained sediment, such as sand, silt, and clay. When a river is blocked by a dam and the current is gone, the sediment in the river settles out and falls to the bottom. Over time the reservoir becomes more a pool of mud than a pool of water. At that point such a dam becomes a white elephant, useless for either irrigation or hydroelectricity. Like other western reservoirs, "Lake" Powell already is silting up and before long it will be a mud wallow. We just do not know when. Those who have examined the Glen Canyon Dam and its reservoir vary widely on its long-term prognosis: Some say the reservoir may fill up with sediment in less than one hundred years; others say it might take several more centuries.

Battered and drawn, the Animas is not unlike other rivers in the Southwest Rockies, stunningly beautiful but pummeled by the forces of human settlement with water diversions, dams, and the environmental legacy of mining. To the north of the San Juan–Animas watershed are two other major tributaries that flow into the Colorado River: the Gunnison River and the Green River. While the Colorado's watershed is shy on rainfall, in its higher elevations it is rich with snowmelt in the Rocky Mountain tributaries, and it is those waters that comprise much of the Colorado River's flow. I have always wanted to fish the Green and someday I might, but at least I was able to get to fish the Gunnison.

North of Durango is scenic US Highway 550 and we drove all the way up there through the San Juan Mountains, fourteeners along the way, including Uncompahgre Peak, the highest point in those mountains. The graceful switchbacks went up and up through the treeless alpine country, and we finally reached Red Mountain Pass, just over eleven thousand feet, about the same altitude as the summit of Oregon's Mount Hood.

Driving on trips in the West allows you to have plenty of time to daydream because in most cases the cities are far between, the distances long, and when the scenic mountains disappear in the rearview mirror, the sagebrush flats ahead can stretch out forever and the drive can become downright numbing. Along such western highways you see all types of recreational vehicles—motor homes, fifth-wheelers, travel trailers—some searching for El Dorado, others searching for a good campsite, maybe at Arches National Park or one of the many canyon land parks in the Southwest. For me, the recreational vehicles on the road can provide entertainment to the benumbed driver because, ironically, the more lavish the RV, the more rugged is its brand name: Bighorn, Cougar, Outback, Wildwood, Hideout, Raptor, Denali, Montana, Eagle, Trailblazer, Kodiak, Warrior, Wolf Pup, Wildcat.

Down from Red Mountain Pass, we finally came to the city of Montrose, the gateway to the Black Canyon of the Gunnison National Park. Incorporated in 1882, the city seemed to be a fine place as we pulled into our motel and began unpacking. I knew next to nothing about Montrose, except for two literary asides: The city was named after Sir Walter Scott's novel *A Legend of Montrose*, and secondly, Montrose is the birthplace of American screenwriter and novelist Dalton Trumbo.

The next day we drove over to the edge of the canyon and I instantly realized that the river below me had been misnamed. As I leaned out over the canyon's overlook, it was as though the very Uncompahgre Plateau had been sliced open revealing an abyss of air all the way to the bottom of the River Styx, the boundary between the Earth and the underworld. This river should have been named the River of Lost Souls.

I gripped the guardrail and tried to comprehend the space below me: The Gunnison River ostensibly was somewhere down there, way down there, a long way down, a half a mile down from rim to bottom, down below the crags, the talus slopes, the sheer cliffs, all the way down to a deeply etched river where the sun seldom shines. In places the river is no wider than forty feet across and the river thunders through a biblical onslaught of fearsome rapids. While the Grand Canyon is the widest canyon in the country and Hells Canyon is the deepest, then the Black Canyon of the Gunnison must be the narrowest. Deeper than it is wide in many places, its rim-to-rim distance is as little as eleven hundred feet wide. At its deepest two Empire State Buildings could be dropped down into that defile, one upon the other, and still have two hundred feet of air on top. I have looked over at the rims of the Grand Canyon and Hells Canyon and was awed by both with the ocean of air spreading across to the far side of their respective rims. But in the Black Canyon of the Gunnison, the rim on the far side is so very close, seemingly right in front of you, as though a good solid drive off the tee could send your golf ball straight into the face of the opposite cliff.

I took my hands off the guardrail and looked away as there was too much space for me to fathom. I blinked my eyes and felt overwhelmed. I looked over at Richard and Bill and Dad. I paused for a few more minutes, collected myself, and then walked back over to the guardrail and looked down again. Way down. The Black Canyon's singular distinction is its dizzying narrow depth, a crack in the Earth's crust that goes down, down a half a mile of space, airily flowing down to the basement of time, the two-billion-year-old Precambrian riverbed of the Gunnison.

Apparently, the indigenous Indian tribes along this plateau shied away from the canyon, and the first non-native person who saw the canyon was a US Army captain named John W. Gunnison who in 1853 explored the area. While he saw the canyon, he did not try to take his party down through the canyon and instead he smartly detoured around the river toward Montrose. Sadly, he was killed a few months later in a skirmish with Paiute Indians in Utah near the Sevier River, though his name became attached to the river that he discovered.

It was several decades later before any adventurous explorers were able to descend all the way down through the river's canyon. However, the pioneers of the Gunnison must have been an especially practical bunch, because soon after they mapped and surveyed the canyon, they started to drill through six miles of hard rock to alter the river. With a force of five hundred men, they created a tunnel to siphon off some of the water of the Gunnison at the upstream end of the canyon and empty it into the neighboring Uncompahgre River to better irrigate its arid valley. Completed in 1909 the eleven-foot by twelve-foot tunnel was one of the earliest projects of the US Bureau of Reclamation. At the time the tunnel was the longest irrigation tunnel in the country.

Back on the rim my hands were still on the overlook guardrail. I looked down into that abyss and said to myself: "I don't think I want to go down there."

But I did.

I did not trip and fall over the rail. Nor did I bravely rappel down those steep, slippery cliffs all the way to the bottom. Instead, later in the afternoon I took our rental car, and my fly rod, and I drove down the one and only route into the canyon, down to what is called the East Portal where the miners bored into the canyon wall to make a tunnel. Even driving a car down into the depths of the canyon was adventuresome as I do not remember ever driving on a paved road that was steeper than the one into the canyon—a grade of 15 percent. In most mountain passes that I have traveled across the West, there are signs on the descending side of the pass to beware of the 6 percent steep grade.

Six percent?

Peanuts, I said to myself as I nonetheless carefully put the car into a lower gear and began to descend. And down I went. I cannot recall how many hairpin turns I navigated but there were many. And at some of the corners, there were round, convex mirrors (like hubcaps) anchored onto the steep banks to forewarn any cars going in the opposite direction.

At last I got to the bottom, parked the car, and assembled my fishing gear. In front of me was yet another lovely Colorado trout river. The locals call it the Gunny. That particular section of the Gunnison is designated as a Gold Medal Water, meaning that there is a possibility of catching a large rainbow or brown trout. The river was clear, very cold, and had rapids, pocket water, riffles, eddies, and pools. It was a walk-and-wade operation because I could not imagine taking a boat down there. I have been told that expert kayakers sometimes run the river down through the canyon. The park's literature warns kayakers that due to the river's hydraulics rescues are impossible. And at high water kayaking should not be attempted period, even by experts. At those times portages disappear and "death is probable," according to one of the more sober warnings in the park.

The river level was low, and besides, I was not planning to get into anything more nautical than my waders. I left the parking lot and went downriver because there was a diversion dam shortly upstream. The ensuing hiking and wading was a bit rough and tumble but not onerous. The cliff walls rising up from the shore to the distant sky made me feel small and inconsequential. Being down at rock bottom in a steep-walled canyon with a dam behind me is always a bit unnerving, but as a fly fisherman, I am accustomed to that risk. Into this chasm I cast out a small dark nymph through a likely riffle, and I could not help myself from craning my neck and looking up at those towering cliffs. Then I slowly looked all the way back down to the river. The riverbed that I was standing upon was formed some two billion years ago, basement rocks, as the geologists say. Those rocks were formed back before the West was the West, back before there were any rainbow trout, back before the dinosaurs roamed. Much of that rock was metamorphosed through heat and pressure, obscuring its very origins. Some of the rock was igneous, too, magma that pushed its way up into the cracks of the Earth's crust where it cooled and crystalized.

At the bottom of the canyon, I also found the riparian zone of life from chokecherries to cottonwoods. At the top of the canyon's rim was a very different flora, its aridity, its pinyon pines, juniper, and withered grasses. And between the top and the bottom of the canyon was a wildlife zoo, because in that in-between country, few people ever go into places such as the Black Canyon of the Gunnison. I looked up at the little eroded flats and along the more gentle banks hoping for mule deer or black bear or even a cougar, but they were not there. I focused back on the river itself and could tell that the trout there must grow fat and old in that canyon because of the quality of the water, its healthy habitat, and its isolation. Some energetic and enthusiastic anglers may claw their way a few miles downriver from the East Portal, but beyond that there must be many places in the canyon where a fish has never felt the sting of a hook.

I continued on casting from spot to spot. It was late summer and by then grasshoppers are usually active, bouncing as they go through the tall grasses on the edges of the river; and when they make one bounce too many, they sometimes end up in the drink. Trout like to eat grasshoppers. Heck, people in many places of the world eat grasshoppers, as well. I was a bit hungry myself as the day was waning, but I tightened my belt and ignored the grasshoppers that I saw bounding through the grass. But I did not ignore the grasshopper patterns in my fly box. I tied one on and greased it up, and I noticed there were more and more rises on the water as I walked along the banks.

Soon I found a large back eddy and cast the hopper out, hoping it would land on a foamy seam and deliver it to a waiting trout. While the air was warm, it was windy and the first cast was off kilter, so I sent the hopper back for another trip. That time the fly floated neatly on the edge of the seam.

The sound of sucking water can mean a number of things to the angler, but in this case the sucking sound where my hopper suddenly disappeared was a good thing. Some anglers call it the toilet bowl flush, as in when you pull down the lever of the toilet and the water in the bowl swirls noisily down the drain. That is what happened on the Gunnison in the depths of the abyss where I found myself one day in early September.

For a moment I did not do anything; I just stared at that big swirl where the hopper had once been floating along. I did not want to jerk the fly away from the fish, but then again I also wanted the fly to pierce the hook sharply into the fish's jaw . . . a beat . . . I couldn't stand it any longer . . . another beat . . . I gave the rod a bit of a jolt . . . not too strongly, but nonetheless there.

Nothing happened. The cliffs were as silent as I was, save the whispering gusts blowing down through the maw of the now-dark canyon. I did not feel the pull of the line, nor the sound of the outgoing line spinning off the reel's spool, nor the bend of the rod and its heartfelt throbbing. I furled my brow—sun-reddened, wind-whipped.

"Where did you go?" I asked the large fish, now hidden beneath the watery film.

There was no reply.

It was a large fish, for only a big fish is capable of creating a toilet bowl flush. Unfortunately, the line was not taut; it was as slack as a line can be. Suddenly, the telltale yellow-colored hopper bounced back out of the film and was floating back down its merry old way letting the eddying currents move it around. While inanimate for sure, if that hopper had some soul to it, it would have been scared out of its mind when that monster of a fish rose up from the depths and tried to attack it. But for some reason the fish begged off at the last moment.

What a fish it must have been: finning in that back eddy, its eyes looking upwards, scanning the horizon for wayward prey, prey that had been washed down the flow and had gotten stuck in a contrary current, maybe a once-carefree grasshopper riding aimlessly on the foam knowing, or maybe not knowing, that beneath the surface there might be a predator lurking about, ready to rocket out from the depths and gobble it up. Some fish, some hopper, some river.

The drive back up the winding, toilsome steep road was at once empty with the loss of the fish, but at the same time filled with a memory of wading out onto a riverbed of basement rocks.

CHAPTER THIRTEEN

Along the Divide: Rivers and Ghosts

TO THE NORTH OF COLORADO ARE SOME RIVERS THAT I HAVE KNOWN since before I was born. My father and his father fished their Montana home waters in the early years of the twentieth century. The waters of those rivers flowed downriver to where I grew up on the banks of the Columbia. Later as an adult, I migrated farther downriver to the lower Columbia where the reach of the tide rises and falls on the River of the West.

I have been back to my antecedent waters from time to time, some with my progeny, some with my forebears, and some with ghosts.

In the states of Montana and Idaho, the landscape is more well watered than to the south of the Rockies: Its rivers are more numerous and larger, and they are fed by more rainfall and snowmelt, plus there are glaciers in the mountains that melt and flow into creeks and rivers, too. West of the Continental Divide, the waters flowing out of western Montana and most of Idaho empty into the Pacific at Astoria. East of the divide, the waters flowing out of eastern Montana empty into the Gulf of Mexico at New Orleans.

In 1805 the Lewis and Clark Expedition paddled up the Missouri River searching for a route over the Rockies and down to the mysterious River of the West. Eventually, they found the three forks of the Missouri's headwaters in south-central Montana. They named the western fork for President Thomas Jefferson; the eastern fork was named after Treasury Secretary Albert Gallatin; and the central fork was named after Secretary of State James Madison. The Corps of Discovery traveled up the Jefferson, over the top of the Continental Divide at Lemhi Pass, and then eventually north toward what became known as Traveler's Rest, not far from present-day Missoula. Then those sore, hungry, and tired explorers hiked over the rugged Lolo Pass and descended down to the Clearwater River, a tributary of the Snake River, which, in turn, flows into the Columbia. There they met the Nez Perce tribe whose members befriended the starving men and one woman and nursed them back to health.

Seventy-two years later many of the Nez Perce tribe were unhappy with the reservation that they were expected to live on because that "painted land," as some called it, was a fraction of their once ancestral lands. After some armed disputes over the issue, a number of those in the tribe decided to flee to Canada where they could continue to roam free as hunters and gatherers. With an estimated 750 men, women, and children and an even greater number of horses, they headed up the trail of the Clearwater River and then up the Lochsa River all the way to Lolo Pass at an elevation of 5,235 feet. It was a trail they knew well, for that is where they often went to hunt buffalo east of the Bitterroot Mountains. The Lolo Trail, however, was not an easy one as the route was steep and thickly forested. Behind that band of Nez Perce was the pursuing US Army, its cavalry, wagon trains, artillery, and hundreds of horses.

Eighty-five years later a brand-new paved highway, US Highway 12, wound its way over Lolo Pass going from Lewiston to Missoula. Some two decades after that, my young family and I drove along that same highway and camped and fished on the Lochsa River. It was a bucolic time for us, a far cry from the privation and unimaginable hardship of the retreating tribe back in 1877—ever tired, always hungry, the bluecoats only a few miles behind them.

The Lochsa is a dream of a trout stream, absolutely clear and clean, its banks thinly forested, the campground nearly empty, the wildlife robust with owls at night and moose browsing along the shore in the morning on a nearby pond. I, of course, had my fly rod along and was hoping to hook up with some west slope cutthroat trout, which people had told me were easy to catch. Well, I cannot recall exactly who told me about the easy-to-catch business, because those fish were not easy to catch. I did hook a few, but it was with great effort. I could see the fish in some areas of the river, but getting a fly to them without spooking them was another matter.

Mostly, I remember the clarity of the water. It was in the middle of the summer and I was wading wet. In some places the river was small enough that you could manage to wade across. I found such a spot where there was a good spot over on the far side and I started to wade across. As I looked into the water, it appeared that there was no water there at all, just a watery lens of some type between me and the cobble bottom, a spectrum of smooth, colored rocks like an artist's palette spreading across the riverbed. I had expected to wade into the river about knee deep and then wade back across to the other side. Well, I kept wading in deeper and deeper. I had no sense of the river's depth for the water seemed more like air than water. By the time I reached up to my hips, I had difficulty standing erect due to the current. The far side of the bank was still far, and I had to turn around. For all I know the water might have been ten feet deep—maybe deeper. All I knew was that if I wanted to wade across the river I better find a better ford.

I do not recall the flies that I used that day. It was in my early years as a fly fisherman and so most likely I had the rudimentary complement of western flies such as an Elk Hair Caddis, an Adams and a few nymphs, maybe a Gold Ribbed Hare's Ear or a Pheasant Tail. Actually, I probably should have stuck with those basic patterns all along, for today I have more than a dozen fly boxes stuffed with all manner of flies and I am not sure if I am catching any more fish now than I did decades ago. Most of those flies I have tied myself, but sometimes I open up a fly box and cannot recognize my own flies and how I once tied them. Like spring cleaning at home, I try to re-organize my flies every now and again and make some order to it. It is always an effort. Before getting on the water, I have forced myself to limit that surfeit of tackle that I too often carry around in my fishing vest. Actually, I seldom use a vest anymore because there are too many pockets in a fishing vest, and wherever there is a pocket, you naturally want to put something into it. I now use a fanny pack that allows me only two fly boxes, pliers, nipper, strike indicators, split-shot, floatant, leader spools, and a knife. Sometimes, of course, I do wish I had a certain fly in front of me instead of having it tucked away back at camp, but most of the time I do not miss it.

At another time and at another place, I also bumped into the Nez Perce Trail. After crossing Lolo Pass the Nez Perce went south and east, and a few weeks later they ended up on the banks of Henrys Lake, a few miles from the Continental Divide. After they left and went off toward the Yellowstone country, the cavalry arrived and they camped on the shore of the lake, too.

A little over a hundred years later, I slept in a comfortable bed at a friend's cabin on the banks of Henrys Lake almost exactly where the two hostile parties had camped. At 6,472 feet Henrys Lake country has an arctic feel to it for the land and waters are frigid for half a year, and the year-round residents are a tiny fraction compared to the large population of summertime vacationers and anglers. I visited there at Tad's cabin several times over the years. I fished on the lake itself, the river that flows out of that lake called the Henrys Fork, and at another river just over the divide, called the Madison, a tributary of the Missouri.

On the day when we went to the Madison, I noticed that it did not take us long to drive from the lake to Raynolds Pass. There we left the state of Idaho behind and entered the state of Montana and the towering Madison Range nearby. The upper Madison's valley was dotted with pronghorn, their tan and white coloring striking as usual. The Madison itself is a hurly-burly sort of river, good stonefly water with broken water, boulders that create pockets where stonefly nymphs lose their grip on the riverbed rock, where large rainbows and brown trout lie in wait just downstream of the nymphs that drift by, helplessly until they once again can put their little legs back on the bottom.

The day I went there, the fishing was fine, the scenery magnificent, but the catching was lean. I did finally catch a large brown trout, but for some reason it was not energetic and almost swam over to me, as though it was asking me to get that damn hook out of its mouth. I have had this situation before with large brown trout from time to time but almost never with rainbows. Sometimes I have thought that some of those big, old trout have figured it out with this sport-fishing business. I call them

Gandhi Trout. They have been around the block and "know," in a way that only fish understand, that their encounters with large two-legged predators are uncomfortable, but seldom fatal.

Why bust yourself? Just go along to get along?

Maybe those big browns understand the principal of passive resistance—Satyagraha.

The big brown waited patiently for me to unhook it and then it slowly swam away. I could have bragged to myself, and to others, about the size of the fish—almost twenty inches long—but I did not do so because it would be a hollow victory. The point of catching a big fish is to hook a strong, fighting fish, one that cleans your clock, as the more aggressive anglers would say.

(Speaking of aggressive anglers, I have noticed recently something called "extreme fishing" in magazines, television programs, and videos. I have seen shots of anglers leaping off surf-pounding rocks in pursuit of fish and others who manhandle three-hundred-pound monsters in faraway places. Those action videos show an "extreme" angler up to his elbows in the river, a rod as thick as a broomstick, the guy busting his guts, filled with adrenaline and testosterone. He—and it always is a he—says that he is a smack-down kind of guy, a lip-ripper of fish. He carves up the river like an assassin and throws out his fly on the water and says presciently: "Just hold on, buddy! That sorry little fur and feathery son-of-a-bitch will soon be nothing but macramé! Sting 'em! Haul 'em in!" I have seen some of those men on the water—and in the fly shops—and it is not pleasant to watch or listen to them. For starters they should switch to decaf. Oh well, it all may be great fun, but it sure is a long way from the pipe-smoking, tweed-jacketed, professorial fly fisherman of yore.)

But back to Henrys Lake. To a fly angler, you do not have to travel far from Henrys Lake for some fine trout fishing, as well as outstanding mountain scenery. Only a rifle shot north of Henrys Lake is the Continental Divide and the Madison. Farther along the east slope of the divide are the Big Hole, Beaverhead, Gallatin, Bighorn, upper Missouri, and the seven-hundred-mile-long Yellowstone River.

Henrys Lake itself is just west of the divide. It is the headwaters of the Henrys Fork, also called the "Fork" by anglers and also called the

North Fork of the Snake River by geographers. That popular fly-fishing river flows 120 miles down to the confluence of the South Fork of the Snake River, which also is an equally popular fly-fishing river.

Just thinking about all the fine trout rivers in that scenic divide country can be overwhelming. I have explored and fished on some of these rivers, but I would need another lifetime to get really familiar with them. Maybe several lifetimes. And they are all different. For example, the Madison is a rollicking type of river with a lot of riffles. A few miles away on the other side of the divide is the Henrys Fork, which is a smooth-surfaced, spring-fed type of river. I have fished both rivers and I have done better with rivers like the Madison. I have never done well on smooth, spring-fed rivers: the fish difficult to catch, even when using thirteen-foot leaders, 6X tippets, and tiptoed stealth on the water. Those silky, smooth-faced streams are absolutely bewitching with their sense of calmness, but at the same time the fish can see you yards away and any untoward movements are instantly telegraphed to the fish. Those rivers usually have a slow current, so the fish can take plenty of time deciding whether or not they might want to chomp down on your fly. In contrast, on rivers such as the Madison, the current is swift with lots of riffles, and as the fly scurries downstream, the fish has to make a snap decision.

So many rivers, so little time. After my reincarnation I will be able to think anew about those waters that I can visit and fish along the divide, but as for the here-and-now, I find myself still haunted by the 1,170-mile Nez Perce Trail and the even longer Lewis and Clark Trail, for at many places along those two trails, I find that their histories and mine inter-sect. After the Nez Perce dropped down from Lolo Pass, they took their immense horse herd, and themselves, in close to the newly found town named Missoula. At the time many white settlers in the Missoula area were frightened of the retreating Nez Perce as they moved down through the Bitterroot Valley, but on the whole there were few altercations as the Nez Perce were trying to move as quickly as possible to escape to Canada and did not want to bother the settlers.

A few years later, in the early days of the new century, my forebears arrived in Missoula. The Indian wars were over and Montana Territory had become a state. There my family lived and fished on their home waters well into the twentieth century when eventually they all moved still farther west toward the Columbia. The Columbia has many tributaries far inland and one of them is the Clark Fork, which flows right through Missoula. Not surprisingly, the river is named after one of the two leaders of the Corps of Discovery who spent time on that river. The Clark Fork is the largest river in the state by volume and its largest tributaries are the Blackfoot and the Bitterroot. The Clark Fork's headwaters are near Butte where over a century the impacts of copper mining and smelting fouled the river for decades, not unlike what also happened on the headwaters in Colorado. Nowadays the Clark Fork's health has improved and the trout fishing can be good there. The river flows northwest from Missoula, crosses the Idaho border, and empties into Lake Pend Oreille. There the lake's outlet continues north and eventually empties into the Columbia River near the Canadian border.

Our family's Montana home waters included the Bitterroot River, Blackfoot River, and Rock Creek, all tributaries of the Clark Fork. Time weaves its incessant way back and forth on such waters. My grandfather, whom I never knew, built bridges across Rock Creek in the early years of the twentieth century. He and later his sons fished on that perfect little trout stream, the bald river rocks crusted with what they used to call periwinkles and what we now call caddis case-makers, little gravel-built shelters that house the caddis larvae. There in the Roaring Twenties, those anglers used their inexpensive bamboo rods, reels, and catgut leaders to catch the wily trout. The trout—Dolly Varden, rainbows, west slope cutthroats—were dropped into an open hole in the lid of a willow-woven creel cushioned with wetted grasses. From the bottom of the damp grass were more than a dozen eyeballs staring at you when you opened the lid of the creel.

Back at home the slippery, silvery fish were dusted in flour and fried in butter in a cast-iron pan, the delicate pink flesh of the river coming forth from lifeless raindrops. Those raindrops became alpine rivulets, headwaters, incubators of life with little more than microscopic bacteria in their clear, cold flow; and down the slope it went, down, down to the rich soup that is the stuff of rivers, living waters, its phytoplankton, zooplankton, caddisflies, mayflies, stoneflies, sculpins, trout, whitefish, otters, ospreys, eagles, herons—and anglers as well. A river tells the story of its land—its soil, nutrients, minerals, all entrained with the flow of the living waters. The anglers cast their offerings onto the Earth's watery veins, blue squiggles on the map, all etched into the ravines, gullies, canyons, and valleys of the world of fluvial geomorphology, the interaction between land and running water.

Years later my young family and I traveled to Rock Creek a few days after we left our camp on Idaho's Lochsa River. I had never seen Rock Creek before, but somehow that well-riffled stream seemed familiar—a ghost river, I suppose. I remember taking our old Chevy station wagon down a rough gravel road, maybe crossing one of my grandfather's bridges on the US Forest Service property, where we found a riverside campsite. The ponderosa pines were thick barked as ever and the camp spots were far apart, not crowded as are many other places.

It was late summer and the river was not well watered so I could easily wade wherever I wanted to go because small waters have few secrets, compared to a larger river where the intrepid angler is unable to fish in many places because of the river's depth, its bank-hugging cliffs, its current, and its dangerous rapids. I do not recall which flies I used or how many fish I landed or what we ate for dinner at our Rock Creek camp. Memory has its way of eviscerating the memories of years past, like many raindrops falling into a puddle that later then vanishes into thin air, and you wish you could recapture the sights and sounds and smells of it all—but you cannot. Speak memory, you say. Yet you are unwittingly mute all too often, unable to dredge up that which you would most like to relive. I was new on those waters and relatively new to fly fishing, so I am sure that my catch was lean. However, I do remember hooking several trout one evening and then on another evening being unable to hook anything. I also remember that there were no other anglers on the river, nor any inflatable rafts or pontoon boats floating by as is often the case nowadays.

We had a few days to enjoy the freshness of the country and the river and so we did. Every afternoon it seemed as though the rumbling cumulus clouds gathered darkly and it rained for twenty minutes and then they floated away. At dusk the bats swooped in, weaving and hurling about through the riverine landscape of tall pines and shortgrass meadows. And at night sometimes we heard an owl hoot-hoot and sometimes a coyote's yipping in the cold mountain air.

We never went back and I do not know why. It is a long way from the tides of the Pacific to the backbone of North America. Since then that little picturesque trout stream has been loved to death by people from all over the world. Nowadays there are world-class resorts a short distance away from where my grandfather once fished, where he took out his sharpened jack knife and slit open the trout's belly from vent to gills, running his thumb up the dark red blood vein on the underside of the fish's spine and then washing the pink flesh in the river's cold water and discarding the gills and intestinal track to the delight of the raccoons, minks, and ravens. Back in the day it was catch and fillet, not catch and release. Many decades later came the summer homes, the motels, lodges, fine restaurants, bars, corrals, bicycles, whitewater rafting, gift shops, and fly-fishing lessons. And all these experiences from a century ago to now may all be genuine—except that for some of us the price of admission was but a tankful of gasoline.

Later we returned again to Montana, but not to Rock Creek. This time it was in the early years of the twenty-first century. Our family included my elderly father, and he wanted to visit Missoula, his hometown, his home waters—one more time. We toured the city, and Dad, ever the scientist, showed us that high up on the slope of Mount Sentinel you could see a horizontal wave-cut line that once was the shoreline of Lake Missoula, the huge proglacial lake that covered much of that area at the end of the last ice age. The lake was held in place by a glacial ice dam up on the Clark Fork River near the Idaho border, and when the dam burst there came forth the Great Missoula Flood that emptied the lake—like pulling a drain plug out of a bathtub full of water. Now the ancient lake bottom is filled with farms and buildings and thousands of people surrounding a crazy quilt of mountains: the Bitterroots, Garnet, Sapphire, and Rattlesnake Ranges.

Dad and I took off by ourselves one morning and drove to the nearby Blackfoot River where he and his brothers and father had once fished. Like Rock Creek, the Blackfoot has been loved to death with lodges, summer homes, and fly-fishing guiding operations. The river has a good reputation for fly fishing and the river also was the backdrop for Robert

Redford's hit movie *A River Runs Through It*. We drove through the splendid views of the valley, hard up against the Mission Range, Swan Range, and Garnet Range, a muscular terrain that stretches up and up to the divide. Back in July of 1806, Captain Meriwether Lewis and nine men traveled up the Blackfoot River to the divide and then over the pass. They were coming back east from their winter encampment in Astoria. The trail up the Blackfoot was a well-worn Indian route where the Nez Perce and other tribes traveled to the other side of the divide to hunt buffalo on the plains. As we drove up State Highway 200, I failed to find that ancient trail, but I did see a public access spot on the river called Russell Gates. We parked the car and went down the river with our gear, including an old-fashioned bamboo fly rod formerly owned by Dad's older brother.

Dad did not feel well enough to do much fishing himself, so I put on my waders and rigged-up the ancestral Montana rod and my own reel and line. We put a folding chair near the river for Dad to sit in and I walked down the bank to the river. It had a good clip to it and was gin clear. The river was not a large one, but it was too big to wade across so I worked downriver out from the bank and cast out a Prince Nymph. I waded in deep so I was able to reach the far side, for wherever the angler steps out into a river, the best spot always, always, is on the far side. The water was frigid even though the summer day was warm. The water around me was transparent and I was able to penetrate its mysterious environment right down to its stony bottom. Standing on the bed of the river, half out of the water and half in the air, I began feeling that I was part of it, the river's current pinned against my legs, my wading boots gingerly dancing across the cobble floor. If I went in any deeper, the buoyance of my waders would have caused me to float and I might have drifted down the river, thrashing, flailing, trying to get back on my feet. So I just took one baby step after the next downriver, stumbling a bit every now and again. Gradually, the wading got a bit easier and I began feeling that I was, indeed, part of the river as much as it was a part of me. Swirling around me were threads of water from the high divide, from Rocky Mountain thunderstorms and shriveled snowbanks, their curvaceous white softness contrasting against the hard granite faces, cliffs serrated against the tender, blue summertime sky. And the headwater icy threads were drawn downward by the invisible force of gravity, down through the high country into the evergreen thickets, down the steep slopes with cascades and waterfalls, down into the self-same valley with its haystacks and red barns and miles of barbed wire strung from weathered post to weathered post. All those waters flowed by me, a puny obstacle in the path of the incessant current momentarily lodged in the belly of the beast. The current flowed around me and lunged onward, madly, relentlessly, flowing into the Clark Fork and the Columbia and all the way to the Pacific.

I looked back at Dad resting in the shade, the waters flowing down the Blackfoot, flowing around my waders, the water always on the move because a river never sleeps. At last a trout snapped at the fly. It and I tussled in the cold water, the fish struggling, fighting for its life, instinctively as only a fish is capable of, bereft of reason, or so we think, but a life all the same trying to live out its day. We too are hoping to live out our days, trying to stay alive, fighting the darkness of the moonless woods where the black dog lopes along, unhurried but always there. Such is not unlike the river's steady current; it is always there, moving along as your days clip by, filled hopefully with purpose and love. The river rushes down the slope of time, blocked by boulders and deadfalls and at other times running smoothly over the calm waters but still always moving, the river's current, your current, eager to find out what will be around the next bend.

I rose up the rod tip and lifted the fish halfway out of the water and could tell that it was not a large fish, but it was bright and sassy, darting and flashing about in the crystalline waters. I could not tell if it was a cutthroat or a rainbow, but I could tell that it was not a brown. And before I could land it and see it clearly, the trout threw the hook, and that was just as well for I was not going to keep it anyway and end its life—not then.

I climbed back up the bank and walked back to where Dad was sitting in the chair under the large ponderosa. I sat down at the picnic table and had a drink from my water bottle and we talked about the big sky country, saying nothing in particular, just the two of us looking out at the divide and our antecedent river, our ghost river. When you go away from a place and its people, you never lose it, or them: They are there, in memory, place and people fused, welded like steel, some of which is visible and some invisible—indivisible for sure.

Acknowledgments

WHILE A BOOK MAY APPEAR TO BE SOLELY THE AUTHOR'S ACCOMPLISH-
ment, in reality there are a number of people who have made this book
possible. First of all, I am indebted to my parents, who steered me in
the right direction from the get-go, especially my father and his love of
rivers, fishing, and the geography of the West. Secondly, I have to thank
my wife, Dyann, and our two children, Michael and Natalie, for their love
and care without which I would be lost.

I have been fortunate to have had many good companions on the
trips that I have made to these western waters, including my immedi-
ate family, my father and two brothers, Dick Mace, Bill Bakke, Christy
Wyckoff, Mike O'Bryant, Vance Thompson, Bill Compton, Don Doud,
Alan Rosenfeld, Mark Skolnick, Fred Ash, John Judy, Rick Hafele,
Brian Lockett, Jon Golobay, Tad Sweet, Larry Baxter, Ray Funkhouser,
Michael Carey, and members of the Portland Anglers' Club.

Another angling friend, Frank Amato, is in my debt for publishing
my work over the years in magazine and book form. I am also indebted to
Kim Koch, who has edited much of my work over the years, including a
draft of this manuscript. Others who have helped sharpen my work over
the years include Barry Grimes, Dave Hughes, Larissa Sweeney, Paul
Albergo, Larry Evans, and Ron Buel.

Stackpole editor Jay Nichols believed in this project from the beginning and I thank him for that very much.

Some may think that because this book has a lot of fishing in it that
it is a fiction book. All the same, I have attempted to write a non-fiction
book, and I have done my best to provide you, the reader, with the most
accurate historical, scientific, and geographical information conveyed in
these pages. Of the more than one hundred sources that I have utilized

while researching this book, I want to especially thank John Harrison at the Northwest Power and Conservation Council, who has provided me with a wealth of information about the Columbia basin.

Finally, my little creation is next to nothing compared to the creation that we have in front of us: our stupendous western landscape, its waters, and its fish. Let us enjoy it wisely.

Index

T

Thompson, David 95

Trinity River 132, 134–35, 138

trout

  brown ix, 38, 42, 139, 168, 170, 175, 182, 183

  bull ix, 157

  Dolly Varden ix, 157, 185

  golden ix, 25, 149–61

  rainbow ix, xi, 14, 22, 23, 38, 47, 49, 53–66, 95, 134, 139, 146, 147, 152, 155, 157, 160, 170, 175, 176, 182, 185, 189

  sea-run ix, 106

  steelhead ix, xi, 3–16, 23, 29, 53, 54, 56, 58–63, 65–66, 67–68, 71, 74–78, 79, 83, 86, 87, 91, 96, 106–12, 113, 121, 122, 123, 126, 128, 135

  west slope cutthroat ix, 180, 185

U

Upper Klamath Lake 132, 134, 135, 139, 140, 145

US Corps of Engineers 53, 91

US Bureau of Reclamation 135, 172, 175

US Department of Commerce 135, 136

US Department of Interior 135, 136

V

Vancouver, George 94–95, 119

W

Washington 8, 14, 58, 67, 89, 121, 131, 136

Willamette Falls 80

Willamette River ix, xi, 19, 79–83, 85, 89

Williamson River 140

Wood River 73, 140, 143, 144, 145